Fuselage Frame Boats

A guide to building Skin Kayaks and Canoes

S. Jeff Horton

Fuselage Frame Kayaks

The methods described in this book are not new. Matter of fact some of the methods used date back hundreds and likely thousands of years. Like all new ideas they eventually become old ideas and seem to fall from favor and are considered obsolete because of their age.

"The farther backward you can look, the farther forward you are likely to see."
Winston Churchill

Looking back there are some really good ideas that still work and work well. In this book I will show you how to build a very lightweight boat for a very small amount of money. Yes, it is possible to build a kayak or canoe that is lightweight, strong, cheap and easy to build.

ISBN: 0615495567
ISBN-13: 978-0615495569

An introduction to the fuselage frame

The word 'fuselage' comes from a French word meaning spindle shaped. It is an aircraft term and the frames used in these boats are similar to that used in airplanes. Building small boats with this method came about with the advent of plywood. Plywood allowed for very light and very strong frames. Thin wood stringers are laid between the frames creating a rigid, lightweight frame. The style was very popular in the 1950's and 1960's and many boat plans appeared in magazines such as Popular Mechanics and Popular Science.

Like most new ideas, fuselage frames eventually fell from favor. However, the fuselage style is still probably the most cost effective way to build a kayak or canoe and I am seeing a renewed interest in this type of boat construction. I attribute this in large part to the Internet. We now have instant access to information that just 10 years ago would have taken weeks if not months to gather if you could have found it at all.

People are rediscovering the advantages of Fuselage style Skin Boats. Building a fuselage frame kayak is fast. From the time I start until I am ready to skin a boat is typically around 45 hours of labor. By the time the boat is finished, I typically have 100 hours of labor invested.

Fuselage frames boats cost very little to build. A sheet of marine plywood, lightweight wood such as cedar for the stringers, a few yards of a synthetic fabric for the skin and something to waterproof it. Materials for a basic 17' kayak cost around $300. Adding a seat, deck rigging and adjustable footrest would add another $100 to $150 depending on your preferences. You end up with a 17-foot kayak that weighs 30-35 lbs. A composite construction canoe or kayak of similar weight would cost thousands of dollars.

I Can Do All Things Through Christ Who Strengthens Me
Philippians 4:13

To my wife Annise, who has patiently let me pursue this path.

With special thanks to my friend Phyliss Crawford who graciously volunteered to proofread and be my editor. Without your help this would not have been possible.

Fuselage Frame Kayaks

TABLE OF CONTENTS

Fuselage Frame Kayaks

CHAPTER ONE

PREPARING FOR THE BUILD

SPEAKING GOOD BOAT

When dealing with boats there are many terms you may not be familiar with. Many of the terms are not needed for building a boat but it is good to be familiar with them.

BOW * front of the boat

STERN * rear of the boat

COCKPIT * area inside a kayak where you sit

COAMING * raised edge around cockpit

GUNWALE * upper edge of the side of a ship

KEEL * bottom center most part (board) of a boat

STRINGER * the long strips of wood that run from bow to stern and are attached to the frames

CHINE * The junction of two sides of a boat

HARD CHINE * a distinct junction as opposed to a rounded over edge

MULTI CHINE * having more than one distinct junction along the sides

ROCKER * the curvature along the keel of the hull

OVERALL LENGTH * length of a boat between the extreme ends

WATER LINE LENGTH * the length of the boat at the water's surface

Multi Chine   Single Hard Chine   Soft Chine

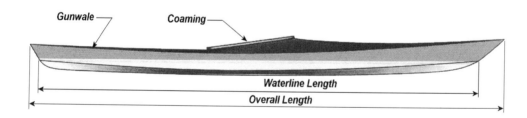

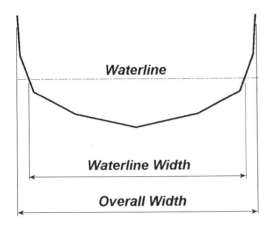

Waterline

Waterline Width

Overall Width

OVERALL WIDTH * width of a boat between the extreme edges

WATERLINE WIDTH * width of the boat at the water's surface

DRAFT * the depth of the boat below the surface of the water at a given Displacement

DISPLACEMENT * the weight of the water a floating object displaces. This is also equal to the weight of the boat. If a kayak weighs 250 lbs total, it will displace 250 lbs of water

The following are some terms that you will often see used that are not a part of boat building:

WEATHERCOCK * this term usually describes boats that have a strong tendency to turn into the wind.

A well-designed boat will turn into the wind if you do nothing but it should be balanced enough for you to easily overcome this and paddle any other direction in most conditions.

Boats should turn into the wind if you quit paddling. If it turns away from the wind when it comes sideways to the waves there is a much better chance of capsizing (boat turning over).

LEE COCK * the opposite of Weathercock. The boat will have a tendency to turn its stern toward the wind. This can lead to a dangerous situation and is an undesirable trait in a kayak

LEAN TURN * it can mean different things to different paddlers but it refers to making the boat turn by leaning it to one side. Some boats will turn easily by just leaning it over on one side. Some will turn better or faster if you lean and paddle.

SHOP SPACE AND TOOLS

Before you decide on what boat you want to build you should look at where you are going to build it. Most people build in their basements or a garage. How much space you have will have a large bearing on what boat you build.

Something a lot of people do not consider is you need room to walk around the ends of the boat. Building a 17' boat in an 18' space is possible but it would be very frustrating. You need enough space to be able to walk around the boat comfortably. You don't want to be constantly stooping under the boat or squeezing by the ends. You will walk around the boat hundreds of times before it is finished. Having enough space to work comfortably could mean the difference in finishing and getting frustrated and walking away.

You don't have to have a covered space. Many boats have been built outside in the open, under a tree or in makeshift sheds. I once rebuilt a wooden Chris Craft Sea Skiff under a temporary shelter I made from PVC pipe covered with a blue tarp.

Another thing to consider is where you will store your tools as you work. A bench placed parallel to the boat will keep your tools near your boat. However, half the time you will be on the other side of the boat and the tool you need will always be on the other side of the boat on the bench.

What I prefer is a set of dedicated stands that places the boat at a comfortable height and has a shelf under the boat. By placing your tools on the shelf under the boat, you can always reach them, regardless what side of the boat you are on. On my stands I place an old hollow core door on the braces and use that as the shelf.

TOOLS

Fuselage frame boats do not require a lot of tools in order to build. It is hard to say exactly what you will need because everyone works differently and has a different comfort level as well as personal preferences. I want to mention some of the tools I

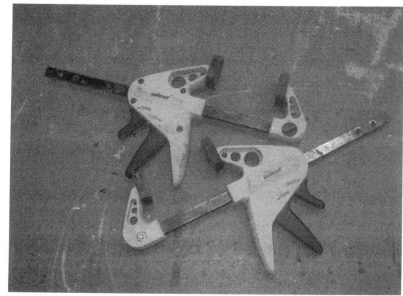

Pistol grip clamps

think are most needed.

You will need some sort of clamps to build your boat. One I consider essential may surprise you, 24" long bungee cords. I find these indispensable when I start to assemble the frame. I consider four to be the minimum and I usually have an assortment of others sizes handy.

Another very useful clamp is the quick acting pistol grip clamp with rubber faces. I really like these for pulling the ends of the stringers together. The rubber faces keep them from slipping and coming loose.

You're going to need a way to measure the positions of the frames. A 25-foot retractable tape measure will work well. I also keep a 12-foot tape handy because it is smaller and it fits in my apron pocket.

Carpenters Framing Square is used to make sure the frames are installed straight up and down.

You will need a level to set the frames on the strongback. A basic 3-foot level is a good choice.

A handsaw is another essential item. There are many different types of saws and the main thing is that what ever you use it needs to be sharp. If you have to buy one I would suggest looking at the Japanese style saws. They cut on the pull instead of the push stroke. They have very different tooth patterns than Western style saws and are very sharp! You have to be careful using one not to cut yourself. Unlike the Western style handsaw, just a light touch can slice your skin open.

For cutting the frames a saber saw is a must. This is one tool I don't recommend skimping on quality. A good saber saw can be expensive, but there is a huge difference in a $35 and $125 saber saw.

I struggled with saber saws for years. It seemed I could never get decent cuts. Especially on curved cuts, the blade would always bend to one side leaving my curved cuts with angled sides.

When I finally replaced mine with a quality saw the difference was absolutely amazing! I could not believe how much better the cuts were. Curved cuts were now square! All the cuts were easier and a tight radius was now easy to make. After using a good saber saw you will give your cheap one away.

This is true with the blades too. Once you get a good saw you really should buy quality blades made for cutting plywood.

Wood rasps are another essential item. My favorite is a farrier's rasp. It is large and easy to handle. It has a rough and fine side and will remove a lot of material very quickly. Another useful rasp that is easier to find is a 4-sided rasp. It has a rounded and a flat face with both smooth and coarse teeth.

There are other tools that will be needed, these are just some of the most essential. I will address other tools as needed.

THE STRONGBACK

A strongback is the backbone on which your boat will be built. It is the reference point, therefore it has to be flat and rigid. There are a lot of ways to construct a strongback and I have seen a lot of clever ideas, more than I can possibly cover here.

You can build a simple strongback from construction grade lumber. The one pictured is (3) 2 x 4's that are screwed together using deck screws. Since the main consideration is keeping the top of the strongback flat, you need to start with straight lumber. When you pick your boards, site down the edges to make sure they are not bowed and/or twisted. When you assemble your strongback, lay a straight edge across it to make

Strongback

sure that it remains flat. I like for my strongback to be about as long as the boat I am building.

Even though I use the same strongback repeatedly, I check it before each build. Wood will move with changes in the weather and newly cut wood will often warp so it is wise to check its condition before you start. The one pictured started to warp and I added a 2 x 6 on top and shimmed it as I screwed it down to keep it flat.

I recommend making your strongback about the same length as the boat you are building. If you think you will be building another boat, you may want to make it longer so you can use it on the next one.

Fuselage Frame Kayaks

SETTING UP THE STRONGBACK

To set up the strongback you need to have made your brackets that you will mount the frames to. These are specific to the boat you are building and you will find the dimension for these in Chapter 5.

I make mine from 1/2" plywood scraps left over from cutting the frames and attach these to a piece of 2 x 4. I cut the pieces of 2 x 4 at least the width of my strongback and I usually leave them a little longer.

Attaching the bracket to the base

To attach the brackets to the 2 x 4 blocks I like to clamp mine to the block and drive in one screw and then check it to make sure the slot is square with the face of the strongback.

Once the bracket is square, I drive in three screws. Drywall screws will work and that is what I am using in the photos. I prefer deck screws with either square drives or torx (star) drive heads. The heads don't round over as easy or break like drywall screws will.

Checking alignment of the bracket

SETTING THE BRACKETS

Once you have all your brackets built you need to attach them to the strongback. I use deck screws with the star drive heads and drive three or four screws through the 2 x 4 into the strongback.

First step is to determine how far apart the frames are, using the chart in Chapter 5. I start by attaching either the bow or stern bracket to the strongback. Then I attach the other bracket at the other end of the boat making sure the distance between them is right. I use a square to make sure the bracket is square with the strongback. This is why it is important to have a straight strongback.

It is very easy to make a mistake with the spacing of the brackets. Keep in mind which side of the bracket the frame will mount and always measure to that side. It's very easy to forget or get confused and measure to the wrong side of the bracket.

How you orient the brackets on the strongback doesn't matter. You can turn the 2 x 4 base block to the inside or outside. Either one will work. I like to turn mine so the block is on the opposite side of the frame it is going to be mounted on.

Once you're sure they are in the right place, clamp , and drive the screws into the strongback and double check that everything is still correct.

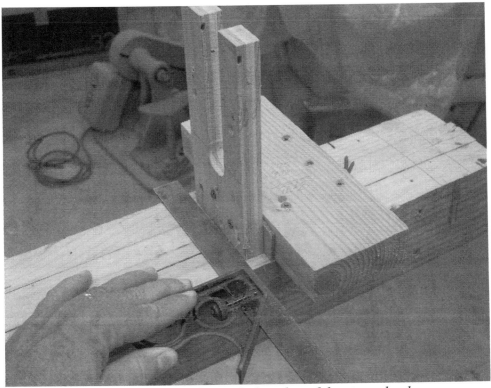

Squaring the bracket with the edge of the strongback

With the two end brackets in place you need to install the center brackets. In order to keep them aligned and not end up with a twist in the keel I stretch a string between the two brackets through the slot for the keel. Make sure that string is touching the same side of both slots. Pull it tight and tie it off. Now you have a straight edge to work from.

As I locate the remaining brackets I make sure that the slot just touches the string and that they are square to the strongback. As long as they are just touching the string (not pushing on the string) I know they are in line.

Once all the brackets are in place, double check the spacing. Make sure they are square, and straight up and down with the strongback.

Fuselage Frame Kayaks

CHAPTER TWO

BUILDING THE STRINGERS

STRINGERS

The next step is cutting the stringers. Stringers can be cut from most any wood but obviously some wood species are better than others. There are some things to keep in mind when choosing your wood. Since one of the joys of a skin boat is its lightweight, you should use a lightweight wood. You need wood that has good rot resistance since your frame will get wet and the faces that have contact with the skin will dry very slowly. The ability of the wood to bend is another consideration. You don't want something that is brittle or breaks easily.

Western red cedar, yellow cedar, cypress and redwood are good choices because of their light weight and rot resistance. This doesn't mean you cannot use other woods. There are other suitable woods and a lot depends on what is available in your area.

It is preferable to use wood that is clear (free of knots and defects) and has a straight grain pattern. Straight-grained wood is less likely to break when you bend it.

Stringer sizes will be different for different boats so you will have to determine the size from your plans and cut accordingly.

CUTTING STRINGERS

Stringers can be cut several different ways. My preferred method is to use the table saw. I start with wide boards that have been planed to the proper thickness, then rip the boards into the proper width strips.

You could cut your stringers on a bandsaw, which is considered a safer machine than a table saw. Many people cut stringers with a hand held circular saw using a guide to assure the proper width. What you use does not matter as long as your stringers are the proper size.

Cut your stringers long. You want to have them longer than you actually need so you can trim them on the boat. If you leave them at least a foot longer it will give you a second chance if you are not happy with the fit at the bow. Plus the cut offs can often be used in other parts of the boat.

Because of the long lengths needed the odds are you will not find lumber long enough to make your stringers in one piece. Therefore you will need to splice the stringers to the proper length using scarf joints.

SCARF JOINTS

In my area it is hard to find any suitable boat building lumber. Finding clear wood (no knots or flaws) long enough for stringers is getting harder and harder. Even if I can find boards long enough, odds are it will have knots. Knots create a weak point in the wood. The way I deal with knots is to cut them out using a scarf joint and glue them back together.

A scarf joint is a shallow angled cut on a stringer with a mating cut on an adjoining piece. The purpose of the shallow angle is to provide a large surface area for gluing. This makes a very strong joint and it is commonly used in boat building.

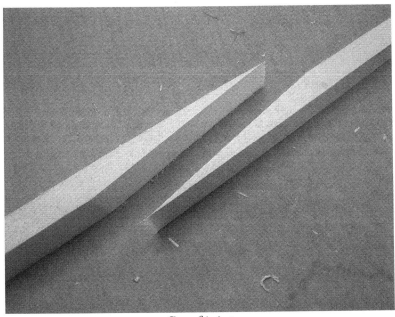
Scarf joint

Because of the difficulty in finding good quality lumber I have developed a good relationship with a local lumberyard and I check the stack regularly and buy anything suitable whenever I find it. I put it in my lumber rack and then I have it when I need it.

SCARF JIG

There are many ways to cut a scarf joint. One of the keys to good joints is consistency. The faces on your cuts have to mate very well or the joint will fail. For best results you need a method that will produce consistent and repeatable results. I made a jig that holds the stringer in the same position for each cut to use on the table saw.

If you have a disk or stationary belt sander you can make a jig to guide the

Scarf jig for table saw

parts into the sandpaper at the proper angle. You could make your own miter box and use a handsaw. I have seen jigs made for a powered miter saw. There are a lot of ways to do these but always keep safety foremost in mind!

If you decide to use a table saw, the jig you use must never trap the cut off piece between the blade and the fence on the jig and you should never let your hand be in line with the blade. A small cut off piece can be sucked into the blade, picked up and hurled at you with great force. I know because it happened to me. It was just a case of my hand being in the wrong place at the wrong time. But it could have just as easily been my face or my eye. After that I set out to design a safer scarf jig for the table saw.

GLUING THE SCARF JOINTS

Tools needed

- At least two clamps for each joint
- Something straight to help align the joint (A piece of scrap wood works well)
- Waxed paper to go between the stringer and the block to prevent gluing them together
- Waterproof glue

Line up all the parts on a flat surface making sure they fit properly before applying the glue. Because of the length of the stringers I find it best to do this on the shop floor.

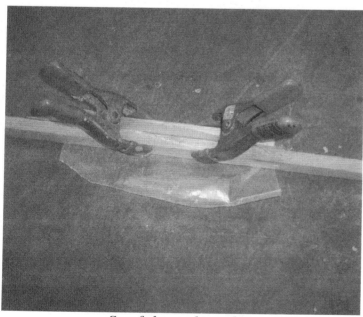

Scarf clamped together

I place a straight piece of scrap wood behind the joint, placing wax paper between the joint and straight edge to prevent gluing the two together.

Apply glue to both pieces of the stringer and spread it evenly. ***This is not the place to skimp on glue!*** You don't want glue going everywhere but you do want enough that when you clamp them together you see some 'squeeze *out'* along the joint. If you don't see glue squeezing out there is a good chance of having dry spots in the joint. More is better here but don't go overboard. You will have to clean up the excess glue later.

Clamp the joint and let it dry. Making sure the wax paper is BETWEEN the stringer and the straight edge you're clamping to. Otherwise, you're going to glue them all together. Since the glue makes the joints slippery, clamp the joint and do not disturb it till the glue is dry or else the joint may slip and have to be redone.

You can make some cheap clamps from 2" or larger diameter PVC pipe. Cut it in approximately ¾" long sections and then cut one side. They are perfect for clamping stringers and other smaller parts.

Fuselage Frame Kayaks

CHAPTER THREE

LOFTING THE FRAMES

UNDERSTANDING COORDINATES

The hardest part of building a fuselage frame boat for most people is laying out the frames. The first thing you have to do is understand the coordinate system. This is how boats are usually designed and how the frames will be dimensioned.

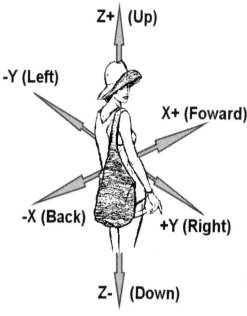

Most designers will provide a Table of Offsets from which you loft (draw or layout) the frames. The dimensions for the frames are typically given in a coordinate system of X, Y and Z locations.

X, Y and Z all refer to a direction and this direction is measured from the same point in space which is referred to as ZERO.

Looking at the diagram of the young lady you can see how each direction has a letter assigned to it, either X, Y or Z. A negative or positive value will further define the direction.

Using these 3 dimensions of X, Y and Z you can locate a point anywhere in space as long as you know where to start measuring from. The starting point is known as Zero or in X, Y, Z coordinates as 0,0,0

On a boat ZERO or 0,0,0 will typically be at the end of the boat. Z will be in line with the lowest point of the boat. X will be on the centerline of the boat running from left to right. Y would be the very end of the boat and runs along the length of the boat.

Keep in mind that some designers may turn the boat around and may place their 0,0,0 at the bow instead of the stern.

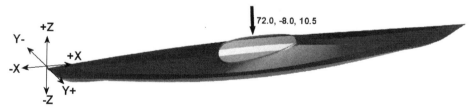

If you wanted to tell someone where the point on the coaming that the arrow is pointing to you would give the coordinate location. In this example we are working in inches. You would start with how far to the end it is, or the X coordinate. Lets say it is 72" so X will equal +72.0. You do not have to put in the '+' symbol, the assumption is that all dimensions are positive unless there is a (-) negative sign.

Next is Y, how far left of the center of the boat the point was. Let's say it was 8" to the side so Y equals −8.0. Negative because is on the left side.

Now we just need the height or Z, and we would know exactly where the spot is. Since it is 10 ½" tall the coordinate would be +10.5".

Putting that in the X, Y, Z format the point on the coaming is located at coordinates 72.0, -8.0, 10.5.

This can be a little confusing if you don't normally work with it. The good news is that for the most part you will only need to work with X (Right and Left) and Z (up and down) when laying out frames. Y will tell you where to place the frames when you start to assemble the boat's frame.

TABLE OF OFFSETS

In Chapter 5, you will find the Table of Offsets for Curlew, Poco Barta and Stonefly.

For an example, I have created a table for one frame and I am going to walk you through the lofting (layout) process. Different designers will use a different format, but it should contain the same information.

X	Y	Z
12	0	1 9/16
	1 5/16	2 15/16
	4 12/16	8 5/16
	0	8 13/16

The X dimension of 12" can be ignored for this step. It means that this frame is located 12" from the end of the boat. That is important when you are installing the frame but is not needed to lay out the frame other than to mark the frame so you will know which one it is when you start to assemble it.

LAYING OUT THE FRAMES

Now you are going to apply what you just learned about coordinates. When laying out the frame on the plywood you will need a long straight edged square, a carpenter's square works well. I use it to line up with the edge of the plywood and I draw a line at 90 degrees to the edge of the plywood to represent the centerline of the frame.

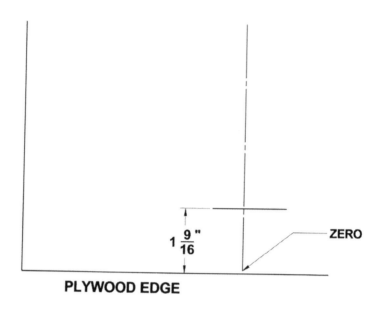

PLYWOOD EDGE

Then I mark my Zero point. To keep it simple I use the edge of the plywood as Zero. Next I will measure up to my first point, using a square and working off the edge of the plywood. In this case I am going to mark the point located at **12, 0, 1 9/16**. As I said before we can ignore the 12 for this operation. Zero in the Y direction is the edge of my plywood. So my first point is in the Z direction 1 9/16 inches. I mark a line across the centerline. Where the two lines cross is my first point.

I continue doing this with each coordinate dimension till I have all the points laid out. Then I draw a line between the points like shown here.

Keep in mind that you will need to draw the points on the other side of the centerline so you have a complete frame. I am only showing half to keep the drawings easier to understand.

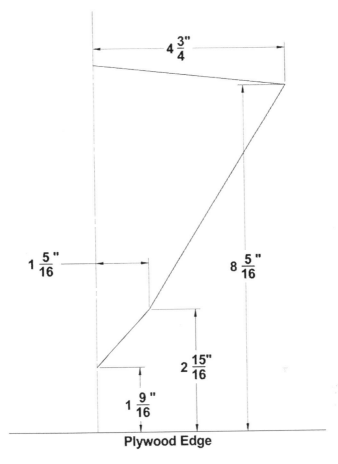

Plywood Edge

The points represent the corners of the boat and the line drawn between them will be approximately where the skin will rest.

Next, I need to draw the stringers so I can cut the notches for them.

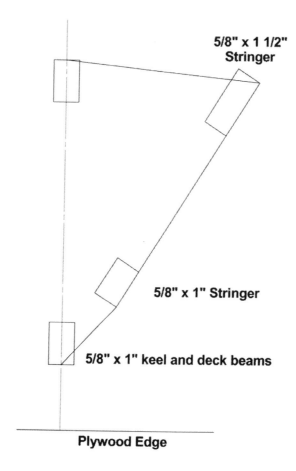

5/8" x 1 1/2"
Stringer

5/8" x 1" Stringer

5/8" x 1" keel and deck beams

Plywood Edge

You need to determine the stringer sizes for your boat. I find it easier and quicker to cut a block of wood the same size as a stringer, or even cut off a small piece of stringer and place it on the frame and trace tightly around it. I line up the stringer on the point and along the edge I drew. As you can see at the keel, gunwale and somewhat at the deck beam it will not line up and will be past the skin, this is normal.

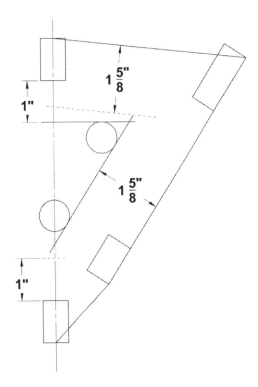

With the stringers drawn in place I need to lay out the inside cutouts on the frame. I like to leave a minimum of 1" of wood between the outside edges and inside edge to ensure the strength of the frames.

I start by drawing a line parallel to the line between points I drew earlier. In this case since I have 5/8" stringers I draw the line 1-5/8" away.

Since the keel and deck stringers are running up and down I also draw a line parallel to them 1" away. At the deck stringer you can see the 1" line is lower than the 1 5/8" line so I want to use that line and ignore the other one.

Since I don't want to use the 1 5/8" line at the top I need to erase it or clearly mark it so I don't get confused and cut to it by mistake. I represent that here by drawing it as a fine dashed line.

At the keel stringer it is the other way around, the 1 5/8" line leaves more material so I would use it and ignore my line that is parallel and 1 " up from the keel.

When I am ready to cut the frames I don't want sharp corners so I drill a hole in the corners with a Forstner bit represented by the circles drawn in the corners. The size is not critical but I typically use a ¾" or 1" diameter bit.

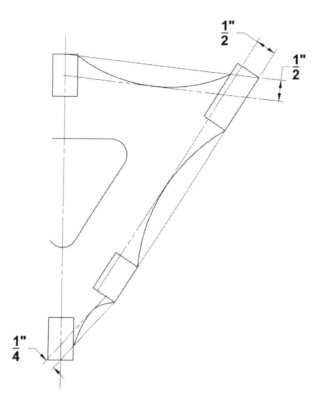

Last step is laying out the relief between stringers. When the water pushes on the skin it will bow inward and there needs to be clearance so it doesn't hit the frames and disrupt the flow of water along the hull.

I draw a line parallel to the outline of the outside of the boat, ½" inch away from the edge. Then I draw an arc. A simple way to do this is drive a couple of finish nails into the plywood, take a thin piece of wood and push it between the two nails to form the arc. Then trace around the wood and mark it on the plywood.

Sometimes on the frames at the ends of the boat the distance between the stringers can be rather small. If I came back ½" to create the relief cut I could end up without enough wood to support the keel. If that is the case I need to do something different such as I did on this example. I changed the relief to a ¼" depth and I changed the shape from an arc to more of an ellipse. This will not present a problem because of the small distance between the stringers. The skin cannot push inward very much and shouldn't hit the frame.

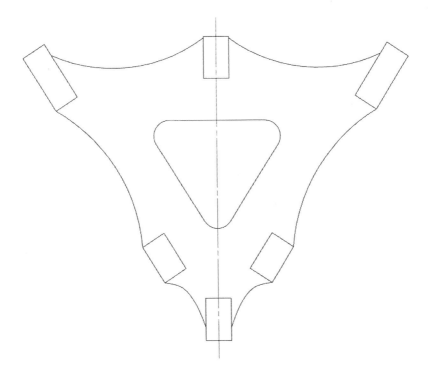

If you did everything correctly, you should end up with something that looks similar to this. You will have some extra lines of course but this is what the final product should look like.

KAYAK FANNY BEAMS

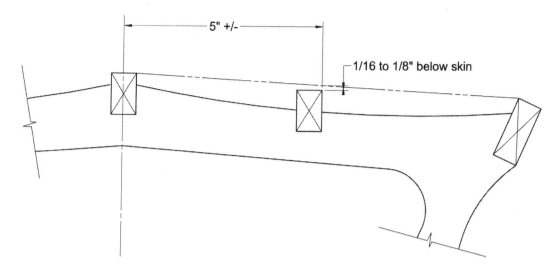

On my kayaks I add two extra deck beams (Fanny beams) behind the cockpit so you can sit on the deck of the boat. These short beams will support your weight instead of the skin.

On all my kayaks I place a frame under the rear of the coaming and another one, approximately one foot behind the cockpit. The purpose of the second frame being so close is for the Fanny beams. The close spacing keeps the beams short and strong.

I cut a notch in both frames on both sides of the center as shown above and place a short deck beam between the two frames.

These dimensions are approximate and you can adjust them if you want, but I have found the 5" spacing works really well. Make sure the beams will be below the skin so they do not show.

REMEMBER! The beams only run between the two frames. The one that supports the rear of the coaming and the nest frame one foot behind that one. They are not needed anywhere else.

- On Curlew these run between frames 4'-4 ½" and 5' 4"

- On Poco Barta these run between frames 5'-6" and 6'-5"

FLOORBOARD NOTCHES

You will need to have something to sit on other than the skin. I have tried a couple of other methods and I have settled on notching the outside bottom of the frames and using pieces of 1/2" plywood lashed to the frames as my floorboards. I use this method on both the canoes and the kayaks.

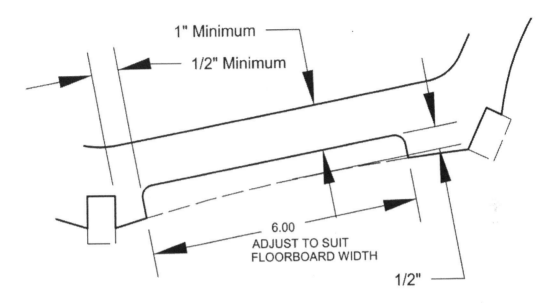

When laying out the frame you will lay out the arched relief for the skin like all the other frames. The bottom of the floorboard will be at the top of the arch. This way you maintain the clearance just like on the other frames.

Mark a line 1/2" above the high point of the arc as shown. Be sure and cut a radius in the corners as shown. Then lay out the inside cutout 1" higher as shown. Do not cut this thinner or you risk having a frame break.

- Curlew floors go between frames 5'-4" and 8'-2"
- Poco Barta floors go between frames 6'-5" and 9'-3"

CANOE FRAME LAYOUT

Frames for StoneFly are laid out in the same manner as for Curlew. There are two things that are different on StoneFly.

CANOE FLOOR NOTCHES

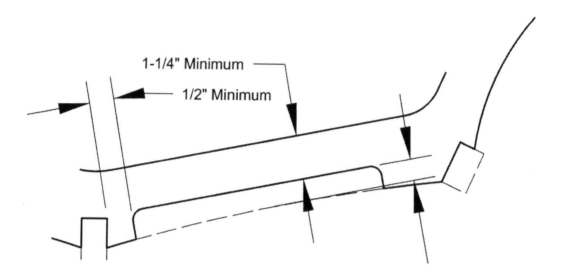

Notches for the floorboards in Stonefly are done exactly as the kayak except that you leave more material above the floors.

You will just have to adjust the width of the floorboards to suit. I installed mine spanning over several frames so that tackle boxes would not rest on the skin of the boat. At the rear of the boat due to space limitations the floors are narrower than at the front. Lay yours out according to your needs.

GUNWALE/INWALE NOTCHES

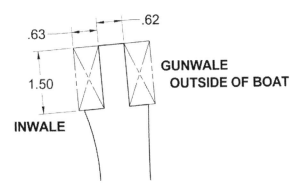

The tops of the frames need to be trimmed for the gunwales. It is important to lay out and cut these accurately so that the gunwales look good when finished. Any irregularities will be very obvious.

FISHING ROD REST

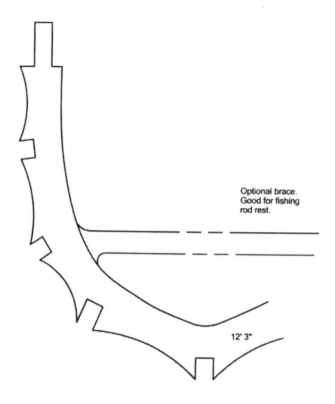

Optional brace.
Good for fishing
rod rest.

12' 3"

If you are a fisherman who likes to carry two or three rods, when you layout the frame located at 12' 3" you should consider leaving a section on frame as shown in this diagram. It provides a rest for your rod tips. Without it the rod tips all end up in the same spot on top of each other. After fishing out of mine just a couple of times I saw what a good idea this would be.

CANOE SEATING

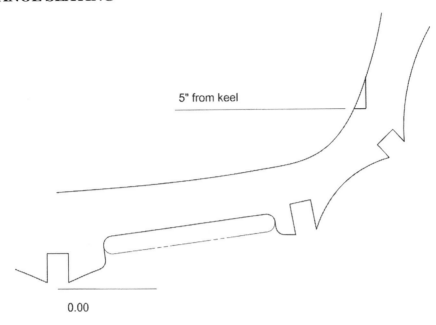

5" from keel

0.00

For StoneFly, you will need to cut a notch inside the frames located at 5'-9" and 6'-9". Lash a stringer in these and mount a seat on top of the stringer. You can make your own seat or you can purchase a wicker seat from several different companies. Trim it to fit and attach it to the rail.

If you prefer, hang your seat in the traditional method off the gunwales. Keep the seat position low or you may find the boat to be very unstable. Lowering the seating position will make a big difference in the feel of the boat.

FULL SIZE PLANS

If you are not comfortable with the lofting process, you can purchase full size plans from Kudzu Craft. You simply spread out the plans and cut out each piece, then arrange them as templates on a sheet of plywood.

Once the parts are arranged I remove each template one at a time, apply adhesive to the back and glue it down on the plywood. I do this to each piece till they are all glued down. Once the glue is dry you can start to cut the frames.

I have tried several different methods of gluing the paper to the plywood and I keep coming back to one product, 3M Super 77 adhesive spray. It may seem expensive at $10-$12 for a can but it is worth the cost. It outperforms anything else I have tried, hands down. Much of what I tried would allow the patterns to come loose as I was cutting the frames, leaving me trying to hold down the paper pattern and cut at the same time. The 3M glue adheres better and is much less likely to do this.

CHAPTER FOUR

CUTTING THE FRAMES

CUTTING THE FRAMES

Frames are cut from 1/2" marine grade plywood. Some people use exterior grade plywood but I don't recommend it. Exterior plywood often has hidden voids between the plies that you can't see until you start to cut it. It tends to warp and overall the quality is not very good. It is generally intended to be used as sheathing and covered with something, such as roofing shingles or siding and not exposed to the weather. If you expect your boat to last a long time it is worth the extra expense for good plywood.

This photo is a good example of why I don't use exterior plywood. This is a piece of exterior plywood that I was going to use to make a mold for laminating coamings around. It has a void in it and the edge curled just a little when I cut it. Next day when I came back to the shop you see what I found.

Example of exterior plywood

I have not tried this but I have heard some people use Medium Density Overlay (or MDO) plywood. It's intended for signs, which are out in the weather. Prices appear to be similar to marine grade so this might be an option.

You can cut the frames using a jig saw. Cut as close to the line as possible but try to leave the line. Remember it's better to be outside the line because you can go back and cut it again, sand it or use the rasp to get it to size. It is always easier to take a little more off than add it back on!

To cut the inside openings in the frames I drill a hole inside and use it as a place to start my cut with the jig saw.

When cutting the slots for the stringers you need a snug fit. You don't want to have to force the stringer in place but you don't want it sloppy either. That is why I recommend making the stringers first. You take a short piece of stringer and check the fit as you make the frames.

Your last step before you start to assemble your boat is to sand the frames removing any sharp edges.

It's not required but I prefer to round over all the inside edges with a 1/4" radius bit using a table-mounted router. This gives a nice finished look and there are no sharp edges to catch anything on. This will also allow the lashing to slide easier and ensure a tight joint.

BUILDING BOW AND STERN ASSEMBLIES

Most but not all of my boats will have a stern and bow that is made of mating pieces that will need to be assembled before being placed on the frame. It is very important to assemble these properly and to make sure that all the parts are square to each other and centered.

If you are building from our full size plans we have drawn them with a tab and slot system to make assembly easier.

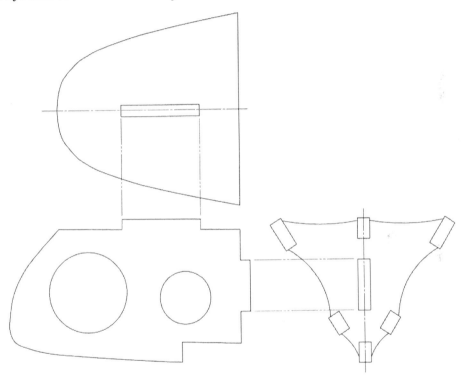

This is an example of a stern assembly. There are three parts and there are tabs on one part and slots in the other two. These fit together and make aligning the part easier.

The offsets do not include the tab and slot. You can add these if you wish but keep in mind they must be accurate or your parts will not line up.

THE FANTAIL STERN

Finding the center line

The stern design is a takeoff of a traditional Baidarka stern. It is original to Kudzu Craft boats and is my own design. It, like the bow, needs to be temporarily assembled so it can be fitted in the frame.

First step is to find the centerline of each part. Measure along the front edge and find the middle and make a mark. Double check by measuring from each side to the line you marked. If it is in the center your measurement from each side will be the same.

Using your square, mark the centerline all the way down the part as shown. Drill two or three pilot holes on the centerline.

Insert your screws and leave just the tips of the screws exposed. I use #6 x 1-1/4" wood screws. Since these will be removed, they are not stainless steel. While you could use stainless steel screws and leave them in place, there is a chance of them backing out and damaging the skin.

Do the same thing with the mating frame and attach all the pieces together. As you assemble these make sure everything is lined up and square with each other. Check all the mating pieces with a square.

Once you have everything looking right, drive the screws all the way in, then back them out and take the assembly apart. Apply glue and put it back together, double check the alignment and set it aside and let the glue dry.

Stern assembly

I can't stress enough the importance of making sure that it is put together right. The stern acts like a rudder and if it is crooked your boat will try to go in circles.

Double check it once you're done and make sure it's right! Otherwise you will end up with a lopsided looking boat or worse, one that wants to always turn to one side!

The bow is assembled in the same manner.

COAMINGS

There are two different styles of coamings I use. One is made from stacking 3 pieces of plywood and the other is laminated from thin strips of wood around a plywood form. Neither is very difficult to make. The laminated coaming does require a little bit of woodworking skill. But cutting three plywood rings that match is not that simple either.

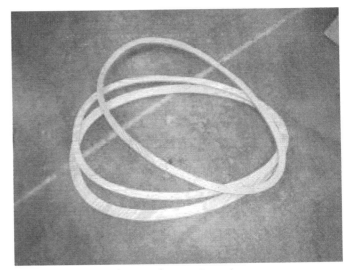
Plywood coaming rings

CUTTING THE PLYWOOD COAMING

Laying out the coaming is very much like laying out the frames. The biggest difference is you have no straight lines; the coaming is just one big curve.

Once you lay out all your points you will need a batten to bend around them. A batten is just a thin strip of wood that bends easily and smoothly. I have had good luck making battens from hardwoods such as oak. The best batten is made from straight grained wood free of knots and flaws. Knots or weird twisted grain may not bend smoothly so you want to avoid them. As for thickness it's just trial and error. Thinner batten will bend more but too thin and it may not bend smoothly.

An example of using a batten being used to draw a curve

Since I work by myself I like to insert some finish nails just outside the points I laid out. I don't put a nail on each point to start with. I put a few in, bend the batten around and see where it falls. If it is close to the points, I start drawing. But usually I will find some areas that are not close so I will add some nails till I get the shape right. If one of the points seems to be wrong, don't be afraid to move it. You want to end up with a fair curve. Sometimes because of the rounding off, the offsets may be slightly off and you will need to make a small adjustment.

I have found small spring clamps to be very handy. You can clamp the batten to the nails. Otherwise you will be constantly fighting with the batten and trying to draw the outline. Trace along the batten and remove it and the nails.

Whether you're working from full size patterns or laying out your coaming from a set of offsets, for the best results cut them a little oversized. Then join the pieces together with a few screws and make the final cut at the same time. It is very difficult to cut three pieces that will mate up evenly and once on the boat it is very obvious when they don't match.

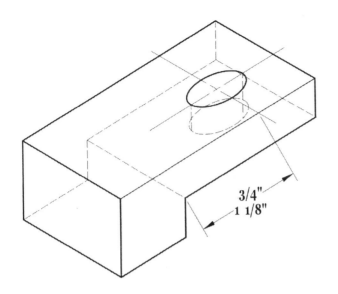

3/4"
1 1/8"

With the inside cut complete it is time to draw the outside edge. I will take a small block of wood and cut it as shown in the diagram. The hole is for whatever I am using to mark with, a pencil or a scribing tool. Since I cut the lower coamings 3/4" wide, I drill the hole 3/4" from the lip. I drill it 1 1/8" form the edge for the top ring.

I let the lip ride on the inside of the coaming and slowly slide it around the coaming marking my outside edge. You want to do this after you have the inside finished.

ASSEMBLING A PLYWOOD COAMING

The plywood coaming is made up of three pieces. There should be two narrow rings and one wider one. One of the two narrow pieces will go on the boat under the skin. (You need to be careful handling this piece once on the boat because it can easily break.) One of the narrow pieces and wider ring are glued together. Check the fit before you apply the glue. Since these are hand cut there will be a difference from side to side. If they don't match, flip one of the rings over and it should match if you trimmed them together as I suggested.

Once the glue sets you will need to lay out the screw holes. I space the holes approximately every 4" and centered on the lower ring. Clamp the two coaming pieces together and use a 3/32" diameter drill bit to carefully drill through all three rings.

Now you need to drill larger holes in the upper coaming ring only. This is a clearance hole for the screw. When you clamp the upper and lower ring together the screw only grips the lower ring and will pull the two tightly together, clamping the skin between them. Don't use overly long screws or you will have a row of spikes on the bottom that could catch on your clothing, and trap you in the boat in an emergency.

BUILDING A LAMINATED COAMING

The laminated coaming is made from thin strips bent around a form. Since it can take a couple of days to make, it is a good idea to do this ahead of time.

I resaw maple into strips and cut them approximately 3/16" thick and about 1 ½" to 1 ¾" wide. On the first and last strip I cut a long taper similar to a scarf cut on one end. The other ends need to be a square cut so it will mate up with the next strip.

You will need to make a form to wrap the strips around. I suggest it be at least 1" thick. I use two pieces of plywood cut to the inside shape of my coaming. Then cut slots all around the edge so that you can have a place to clamp to. Be sure the slots run around the curves because that is where you need the most clamps.

Sawing the strips

The first strip should be the one with a tapered end. Clamp the tapered end to the jig and start to bend it around the frame. When you get to the curve, heat the strip using a heat gun. Apply a little pressure with the heat and you will feel it relax and bend around the curve with little effort. Add clamps to hold it in place as you go.

When you get to the point that the strip starts to overlap itself, apply the glue. Make sure you use enough clamps to pull the strips tight and see some glue squeeze out of the joint. You do not want any gaps, so watch closely as you work. Keep adding clamps to close all the gaps.

I prefer Titebond III glue for this application because it is waterproof, and it has a long open time, which gives me more time to get everything right before it sets up.

Once the first strip is in place, apply glue to 2 or 3 feet of the next strip and butt it against the end of the first strip. Clamp it and start bending it around the form, clamping it as you go. Continue working all the way around the coaming.

As you add more strips you will find that it becomes harder to keep the gaps closed with just spring clamps. I have found that C and/or F clamps are better choices on the curved ends. You will need the extra strength to pull the laminations tight.

Laminated coaming form

It is a good idea to laminate a couple of strips around the form and let the glue set. After it dries add a couple more strips, building the coaming over several days. I have tried to do them all at one time and the results were not very good.

I make the coaming body at least 1/2" thick, maybe a little more. The last strip you put in place should have a tapered end on it so that it blends into the coaming rather than just comes to an abrupt end. Let it sit overnight before you start on the lip.

COAMING LIP

Once the glue is dry you can take the coaming off the form if you want. For the coaming lip I cut a couple of the left over strips into approximately 3/8"+ wide pieces. Then I glue the lip onto the coaming the same way I laminate the coaming.

It's difficult to glue the small strips on evenly. I work around the top of the coaming because it is much easier to clamp the strips there. I try to line them up as best I can with the top edge of the coaming. I make the lip around 3/8" wide.

FINISHING THE COAMING

Once the coaming comes off of the jig you will have to flatten the top and bottom edges. I often start with a belt sander because it is quick. I clamp the coaming to the bench and use a hand plane and flatten top and bottom edges.

I drill a series of holes approximately 2" apart to stitch the skin on. I mark the spacing on the coaming and I use a simple jig made from scraps to keep my spacing from the top of the coaming consistent.

Drilling the stitch holes

Occasionally I will find a gap along the bottom of the coaming once I remove it from the form. You never want to leave a place for water to enter and be trapped because it can lead to rot.

If I can close the gap with a clamp I fill the gap with some glue, clamp it and let it dry. If that will not work, I fill the hole with 5-minute epoxy. Once it sets, I sand it smooth.

Last step is a lot of sanding and applying whatever finish you want. If you want a natural finish make sure it is an outdoor finish such as spar varnish with UV protection.

Fuselage Frame Kayaks

CHAPTER FIVE

THE BOATS

CURLEW

15' LONG 22" WIDE (4.57 M * 55.9 CM)

Curlew started out as a challenge by a friend to design a boat for the average paddler to use on our local water, the Tennessee River and its large lakes.

Most people talk about the desire to camp from their boats but very few actually do. Since most people rarely carry more than their lunch, a jacket and maybe some extra water we decided a smaller space was adequate. Top speed was not an issue because most people paddle in the 3 to 4.5 mph range. As for water conditions, we have mostly flat water but we can have very closely spaced two foot waves and sometimes three foot in high winds such as a surprise summer thunderstorm. They can come up quick so this was something I wanted to make sure the boat could handle. Using this information we set our design goals.

Once the design was finished, Curlew was 15' long and had an overall beam of 22". I like to call it a fast cruiser because the hull was optimized for the 3 to 4.5 mph range, the speed range most recreational paddlers spend most of their time in. The chosen design speed is how it ended up being 15' long. Any longer and the hull resistance went up at these speeds. Any shorter and it needed to be wider to keep the stability acceptable, which made resistance go up also. The 15' length and 22" overall width was the 'sweet spot'.

After building Curlew I realized there was more space, especially in the back of the boat than expected. If you add a hatch, there is room for some camping gear. There isn't the capacity for an extended trip but if you pack light and don't bring the kitchen sink along there is plenty of space.

The boat responds very well to lean turns. Slight course corrections are quick and easy yet it still tracks very well. Everyone that has paddled this boat liked it.

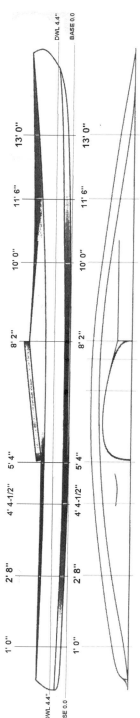

CURLEW FRAME OFFSETS

Dimensions are in Feet and inches

X	Y	Z
1' 0"	0	1 9/16
	1 5/16	2 15/16
	4 12/16	8 5/16

X	Y	Z
2' 8"	0	14/16
	5 3/16	2 4/16
	8	7 11/16
	0	8 6/16

X	Y	Z
4' 4-1/2"	0	5/16
	7 15/16	1 13/16
	10 7/16	7 5/16
	4 2/16	7 13/16
	0	8 2/16

X	Y	Z
5' 4"	0	3/16
	8 13/16	1 11/16
	11 6/16	7 3/16
	0	8 1/16

X	Y	Z
8' 2"	0	1/16
	8 15/16	1 11/16
	11 5/16	7 3/16
	4 4/16	11 15/16
	0	12

X	Y	Z
10' 0"	0	5/16
	6 12/16	2 1/16
	9	7 12/16
	4 4/16	10 6/16
	0	11

X	Y	Z
11' 6"	0	11/16
	4	2 7/16
	6 9/16	8 10/16
	0	10 15/16

X	Y	Z
13' 0"	0	1 5/16
	156	1 4/16	2 14/16
	156	4	9 14/16
	156	0	11 5/16

BOW AND STERN OFFSETS

Dimensions are in Inches

STERN TOP		
X	Y	Z
-9 4/16	0	0
-9	1 6/16	0
-8	2 8/16	0
-7	3	0
-6	3 6/16	0
-5	3 11/16	0
-4	3 15/16	0
-3	4 2/16	0
-2	4 6/16	0
-1	4 9/16	0
0	4 12/16	0

STERN		
X	Y	Z
12	15/16	0
9	1	0
9	0	0
6	3/16	0
3	6/16	0
1	13/16	0
9/16	1	0
4/16	2	0
12/16	4	0
1 6/16	5	0
2 12/16	6 8/16	0
12	6 7/16	0

BOW		
X	Y	Z
0	1	0
3	3/16	0
6	6/16	0
9	11/16	0
12	1 1/16	0
14	1 7/16	0
17	2 3/16	0
19	3 1/16	0
21	4 4/16	0
23 2/16	6	0
24 1/16	8	0
23	10 11/16	0
3	10 1/16	0
3	9 1/16	0
0	9	0

34" COAMING		
X	Y	Z
1	0	0
2	4 2/16	0
4	6 12/16	0
6	8 1/16	0
10	9	0
12	8 14/16	0
15	8 8/16	0
19	8	0
23	7 2/16	0
27	5 15/16	0
31	4 9/16	0
32	4 4/16	0
33	3 12/16	0
34	2 13/16	0
35	0	0

CURLEW FRAME OFFSETS

METRIC Dimensions are millimeters

FRAME 1' 0"		
X	Y	Z
304.80	0.00	39.37
	33.53	73.91
	120.14	211.07

FRAME 2' 8"		
X	Y	Z
812.80	0.00	22.35
	132.08	56.64
	202.95	195.33
	0.00	212.34

FRAME 4' 4-1/2"		
X	Y	Z
1333.50	0.00	8.64
	201.68	45.47
	265.18	185.67
	104.65	197.87
	0.00	206.25

FRAME 5' 4"		
X	Y	Z
1625.60	0.00	4.32
	223.77	42.42
	288.29	182.12
	0.00	204.22

FRAME 8' 2"		
X	Y	Z
2489.20	0.00	1.78
	227.33	42.16
	286.77	182.12
	107.19	303.28
	0.00	304.80

FRAME 10' 0"		
X	Y	Z
3175.00	0.00	7.62
	171.20	52.32
	229.36	197.10
	107.19	263.91
	0.00	280.16

FRAME 11' 6"		
X	Y	Z
3505.20	0.00	17.27
	101.35	62.48
	167.39	219.46
	0.00	278.38

FRAME 13' 0"		
X	Y	Z
3962.40	0.00	33.53
	32.26	73.41
	100.84	250.70
	0.00	287.78

BOW AND STERN OFFSETS

METRIC Dimensions are millimeters

STERN TOP		
X	Y	Z
-234.95	0.00	0.00
-228.60	35.05	0.00
-203.20	63.50	0.00
-177.80	76.71	0.00
-152.40	85.60	0.00
-127.00	93.47	0.00
-101.60	99.57	0.00
-76.20	105.41	0.00
-50.80	110.49	0.00
-25.40	115.32	0.00
0.00	120.14	0.00

STERN		
X	Y	Z
304.80	23.11	0.00
228.60	25.40	0.00
228.60	0.00	0.00
152.40	4.06	0.00
76.20	9.91	0.00
25.40	20.32	0.00
14.73	25.40	0.00
6.60	50.80	0.00
19.05	101.60	0.00
35.56	127.00	0.00
69.85	164.85	0.00
304.80	163.07	0.00

BOW		
X	Y	Z
0.00	25.40	0.00
76.20	4.06	0.00
152.40	9.91	0.00
228.60	17.27	0.00
304.80	27.18	0.00
355.60	36.58	0.00
431.80	55.37	0.00
482.60	78.23	0.00
533.40	107.95	0.00
587.50	152.40	0.00
610.62	203.20	0.00
584.45	270.76	0.00
75.44	256.29	0.00
76.20	230.89	0.00
0.00	228.60	0.00

86.4 CM COAMING		
X	Y	Z
25.40	0.00	0.00
50.80	105.16	0.00
101.60	170.69	0.00
152.40	204.98	0.00
254.00	228.85	0.00
304.80	224.79	0.00
381.00	216.66	0.00
482.60	202.44	0.00
584.20	180.85	0.00
685.80	151.38	0.00
787.40	116.59	0.00
812.80	107.70	0.00
838.20	95.00	0.00
863.60	71.63	0.00
889.00	0.00	0.00

Fuselage Frame Kayaks

These drawings show what the bow and stern offsets should look like once finished:

CURLEW

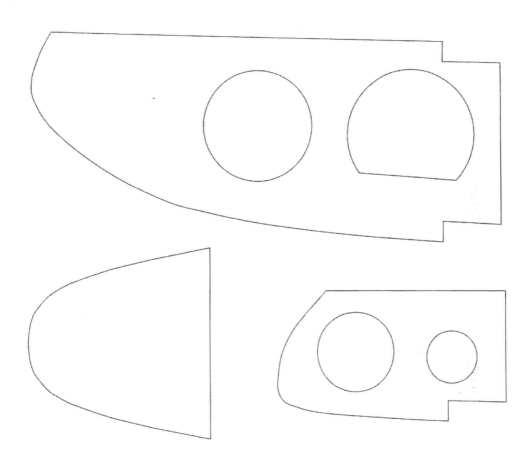

MATERIALS

- Frames cut from ½" (12 mm) marine grade plywood
- Gunwales are 5/8" x 1-1/2" (15.88 mm x 38.1 mm)
- Stringers are 5/8" x 1" (15.88 mm x 25.4 mm)
- Keel is 5/8" x 1" (15.88 mm x 25.4 mm)

CURLEW BRACKETS

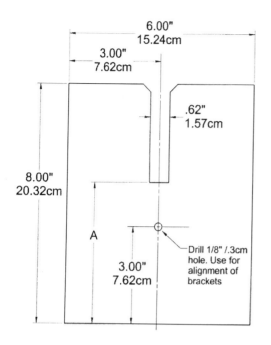

This shows the overall layout for each of the three brackets that attach to the strongback. The brackets locate the frames of the boat in the proper position. Once mounted to the strongback you attach the appropriate frame to the bracket.

The 5/8" wide slot needs to be just wide enough for stringer to slide inside and not stick.

You may find that you need to trim the corners at the top to clear the stringers on the frame.

CURLEW BRACKETS	
BRACKET LOCATION	**'A' Dimension**
FRAME 1' 0"	5-9/16" (141.29 mm)
FRAME 4' 4 1/2"	4-5/16" (109.54 mm)
FRAME 8' 2"	4-1/16" (103.19 mm)
FRAME 13' 0"	5-5/16" (134.94 mm)

POCO BARTA

17' LONG 23" WIDE (5.18 M* 55.9 CM)

Poco Barta looks very much like Curlew but it is not just a stretched version of the same boat. They are similar but they are two different boats.

Poco Barta is a longer boat and compared to Curlew will have slightly higher resistance at the lower speeds but when you pour on the power the longer water line will reward you with more speed potential than Curlew.

Stability is very similar in the two boats and both being hard chines999 they will feel very similar on the water. A little bit of lean and this boat is going to turn so making small course corrections are simple. Tracking will be good but not overly tight.

Poco Barta is not a touring boat but there is enough space to add a couple of hatches and be able to haul camping gear.

This boat will do a lot of things well and will be great multi purpose boat.

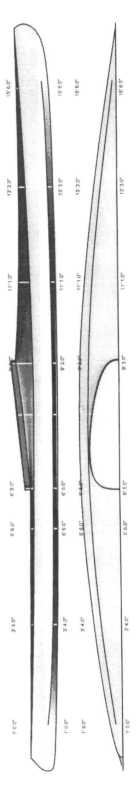

POCO BARTA FRAME OFFSETS

Dimensions are in Feet and inches

X	Y	Z
1' 0"	0	1 7/16
	1 13/16	3 5/16
	3 7/16	8 7/16
	0	8 10/16

X	Y	Z
3' 4"	0	10/16
	5 13/16	2
	8	7 10/16
	0	8 6/16

X	Y	Z
5' 6"	0	4/16
	8 3/16	1 8/16
	10 10/16	7 2/16
	0	8 2/16

X	Y	Z
6' 5"	0	2/16
	8 12/16	1 7/16
	11 3/16	7
	0	8

X	Y	Z
9' 3"	0	1/16
	8 13/16	1 7/16
	11 4/16	7 2/16
	0	11 8/16

X	Y	Z
11' 1"	0	4/16
	7 9/16	1 11/16
	9 12/16	7 11/16
	0	10 15/16

X	Y	Z
13' 3"	0	12/16
	4 12/16	2 5/16
	6 11/16	8 12/16
	0	10 11/16

X	Y	Z
15' 6"	0	1 13/16
	1 5/16	3 11/16
	2 10/16	10 6/16
	0	11 2/16

POCO BARTA BOW AND STERN OFFSETS

Dimensions are in inches

STERN TOP		
X	Y	Z
3 9/16	0	0
4	1	0
5	1 9/16	0
6	1 15/16	0
7	2 4/16	0
8	2 8/16	0
9	2 12/16	0
10	3	0
11 12/16	3 6/16	0
11 12/16	0	0

BOW		
X	Y	Z
0	0	1 13/16
4	0	2 3/16
8	0	2 11/16
10	0	3 1/16
12	0	3 9/16
14	0	4 7/16
16	0	6 3/16
17	0	7 10/16
17 3/16	0	9
16 15/16	0	10
16	0	11 9/16
0	0	11 2/16

STERN UPRIGHT		
X	Y	Z
11 12/16	0	8 2/16
11 12/16	0	2 7/16
8 12/16	0	2 9/16
8 12/16	0	1 9/16
6 11/16	0	1 10/16
4 3/16	0	1 12/16
1 3/16	0	2 3/16
5/16	0	2 11/16
1/16	0	3 4/16
0	0	4
9/16	0	5 12/16
2 11/16	0	7 15/16
3 9/16	0	8 3/16
3 9/16	0	8 11/16

34" COAMING		
X	Y	Z
1	0	0
2	4 2/16	0
4	6 12/16	0
6	8 1/16	0
10	9	0
12	8 14/16	0
15	8 8/16	0
19	8	0
23	7 2/16	0
27	5 15/16	0
31	4 9/16	0
32	4 9/16	0
33	3 12/16	0
34	2 13/16	0
35	0	0

Poco Barta Frame Offsets

METRIC Dimensions are millimeters

FRAME 1' 0"		
X	**Y**	**Z**
304.80	0.00	36.09
	45.42	83.52
	86.75	214.34
	0.00	219.24

FRAME 3' 4"		
X	**Y**	**Z**
1016.00	0.00	16.43
	147.46	50.87
	202.45	193.73
	0.00	212.35

FRAME 5' 6"		
X	**Y**	**Z**
1676.40	0.00	0.22
	8.21	1.52
	10.62	7.12
	0.00	8.11

FRAME 6' 5"		
X	**Y**	**Z**
1955.80	0.00	3.23
	222.78	36.52
	284.10	178.28
	0.00	203.30

FRAME 9 '3"		
X	**Y**	**Z**
2819.40	0.00	1.80
	223.60	37.09
	286.24	181.02
	0.00	292.00

FRAME 11' 1"		
X	**Y**	**Z**
3378.20	0.00	6.34
	191.87	42.98
	247.25	195.32
	0.00	277.06

FRAME 13' 3"		
X	**Y**	**Z**
4038.60	0.00	18.29
	120.64	59.13
	170.26	222.78
	0.00	271.00

FRAME 15' 6"		
X	**Y**	**Z**
4724.40	0.00	45.93
	33.77	93.12
	66.90	264.14
	0.00	282.24

POCO BARTA BOW AND STERN OFFSETS

METRIC Dimensions are millimeters

STERN UPRIGHT		
X	Y	Z
11 12/16	0	8 2/16
11 12/16	0	2 7/16
8 12/16	0	2 9/16
8 12/16	0	1 9/16
6 11/16	0	1 10/16
4 3/16	0	1 12/16
1 3/16	0	2 3/16
5/16	0	2 11/16
1/16	0	3 4/16
0	0	4
9/16	0	5 12/16
2 11/16	0	7 15/16
3 9/16	0	8 3/16
3 9/16	0	8 11/16

34" COAMING		
X	Y	Z
1	0	0
2	4 2/16	0
4	6 12/16	0
6	8 1/16	0
10	9	0
12	8 14/16	0
15	8 8/16	0
19	8	0
23	7 2/16	0
27	5 15/16	0
31	4 9/16	0
32	4 9/16	0
33	3 12/16	0
34	2 13/16	0
35	0	0

STERN TOP		
X	Y	Z
3 9/16	0	0
4	1	0
5	1 9/16	0
6	1 15/16	0
7	2 4/16	0
8	2 8/16	0
9	2 12/16	0
10	3	0
11 12/16	3 6/16	0
11 12/16	0	0

BOW		
X	Y	Z
0	0	1 13/16
4	0	2 3/16
8	0	2 11/16
10	0	3 1/16
12	0	3 9/16
14	0	4 7/16
16	0	6 3/16
17	0	7 10/16
17 3/16	0	9
16 15/16	0	10
16	0	11 9/16
0	0	11 2/16

These drawings show what the bow and stern offsets should look like once finished:

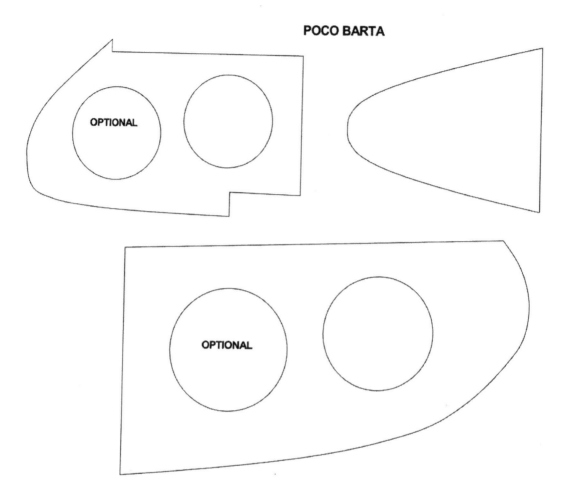

POCO BARTA

MATERIALS

- Frames cut from ½" marine grade plywood
- Gunwales are 5/8" x 1-1/2"
- Stringers are 5/8" x 1"
- Keel is 5/8" x 1"

POCO BARTA BRACKETS

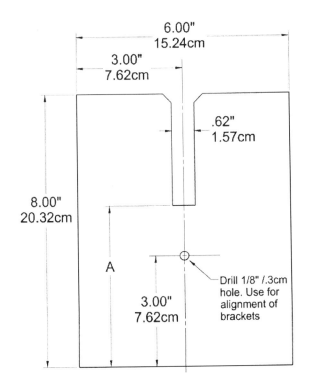

This shows the overall layout for each of the three brackets that attach to the strongback. The brackets locate the frames of the boat in the proper position. Once mounted to the strongback you attach the appropriate frame to the bracket.

The 5/8" wide slot needs to be just wide enough for stringer to slide inside and not stick.

You may find that you need to trim the corners at the top to clear the stringers on the frame.

POCO BARTA BRACKETS	
BRACKET LOCATION	**'A' Dimension**
FRAME 1' 0"	5 7/16" (138.12 mm)
FRAME 6' 5"	4 2/16" (104.77 mm)
FRAME 11' 1"	4 4/16" (107.95 mm)
FRAME 15' 6"	5 13/16"(147.64 mm)

STONEFLY CANOE

14' 9" LONG 29" WIDE (4.5 M * 73.7 CM)

I had been thinking about a skin canoe for a while but I am not a big canoe fan, I just prefer a kayak. But after a few fishing trips in my kayak I started to think a canoe might be better for fishing. It would be more comfortable and it would provide a place inside the boat to put your gear. Plastic SOT (Sit On Top) kayaks designed for fishing are great fishing boats but the weight always turned me off to them. So I decided to build a canoe for fishing.

After finishing StoneFly and paddling it a little bit I was convinced a canoe was a better choice for fishing. It's far more comfortable since you can move around and get to your gear much easier. Rods are stored inside the boat so there is little risk of them being dragged out of the boat (a big consideration on creeks with lots of low hanging branches).

StoneFly is stable and comfortable. Unlike your typical canoe, StoneFly tracks strong. I paddle on a big lake so I may cover a few miles to get to where I want to fish and the tracking is appreciated. You can easily paddle this boat with a canoe paddle without knowing the J stroke. If you're fishing a smaller creek where you may want to spin the boat around quickly it's a big drawback.

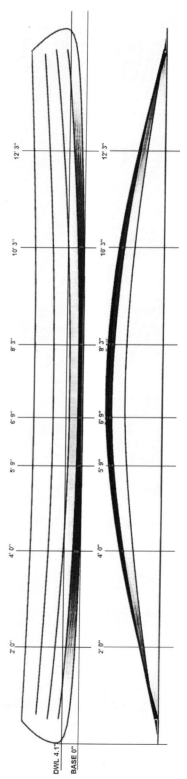

BOW AND STERN OFFSETS

This drawing shows what the bow and stern should look like once finished:

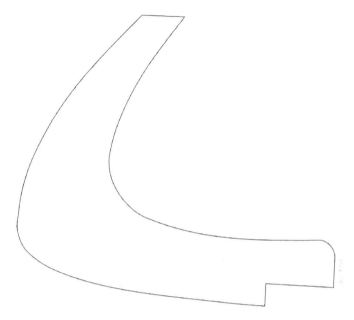

All stringers are 5/8" (15.88 mm) wide

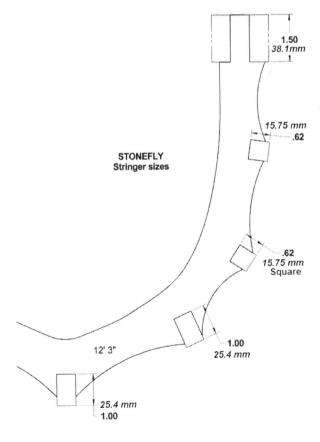

STONEFLY
Stringer sizes

1.50
38.1mm

15.75 mm
.62

.62
15.75 mm
Square

1.00
25.4 mm

12' 3"

25.4 mm
1.00

STONEFLY FRAME OFFSETS

Dimensions are in Feet and inches

X	Y	Z
2' 0"	0	1 3/16
	3 13/16	3 7/16
	4 14/16	6 3/16
	5	9 10/16
	4 15/16	13 12/16

X	Y	Z
4' 0"	0	5/16
	7	2 1/16
	9 8/16	4 9/16
	10	8 6/16
	10 6/16	12 15/16

X	Y	Z
5' 9"	0	1/16
	8 15/16	1 7/16
	12 4/16	3 10/16
	12 15/16	7 11/16
	13 8/16	12 9/16

X	Y	Z
6' 9"	0	0
	9 8/16	1 4/16
	12 14/16	3 7/16
	13 11/16	7 8/16
	14 5/16	12 7/16

X	Y	Z
8' 3"	0	0
	9 4/16	1 3/16
	12 6/16	3 8/16
	13 6/16	7 10/16
	14 1/16	12 7/16

X	Y	Z
10' 3"	0	4/16
	7 9/16	1 12/16
	10 3/16	4 3/16
	11 2/16	8 2/16
	11 8/16	12 11/16

X	Y	Z
12' 3"	0	15/16
	4 9/16	3
	6 5/16	5 10/16
	6 13/16	9 4/16
	6 13/16	13 5/16

Fuselage Frame Kayaks

STONEFLY OFFSETS

Dimensions are in inches

BOW	
X	**Y**
10/16	1 2/16
3 10/16	1 6/16
3 11/16	6/16
6	9/16
9	15/16
12	1 9/16
13	1 15/16
14	2 7/16
14 11/16	4
14 10/16	5
14 5/16	6
13 3/16	8
11 10/16	10
9 2/16	12 13/16
6 14/16	12 11/16
8	11 2/16
9	9 9/16
10 2/16	7
10 5/16	6
10 5/16	6
10	4 11/16
9 3/16	4
7	3 7/16
4	3 3/16
2	3
1	2 13/16
9/16	2

STERN	
X	**Y**
11 4/16	4/16
11 5/16	1 3/16
14 5/16	1
14 6/16	2
13 11/16	3
12	3 1/16
9	3 4/16
7	3 12/16
5	4 14/16
4 7/16	6
4 8/16	7
5 4/16	9
6 9/16	11
7 14/16	12 10/16
5 5/16	12 12/16
4	10 14/16
2	8 7/16
12/16	6
5/16	4
8/16	3
1	2 8/16
3	1 8/16
6	14/16
11 4/16	4/16

STONEFLY FRAME OFFSETS

METRIC Dimensions are millimeters

Frame 2' 0"		
X	Y	Z
50.80	0.00	1.16
	3.84	3.43
	4.88	6.18
	5.00	9.65
	4.96	13.73

Frame 4' 0"		
X	Y	Z
101.60	0.00	0.31
	6.98	2.09
	9.48	4.54
	10.03	8.35
	10.41	12.94

Frame 5' 9"		
X	Y	Z
1752.60	0.00	0.05
	8.93	1.41
	12.24	3.63
	12.94	7.68
	13.50	12.56

Frame 6' 9"		
X	Y	Z
2057.40	0.00	0.00
	9.47	1.22
	12.85	3.41
	13.69	7.53
	14.32	12.45

Frame 8' 3"		
X	Y	Z
2514.60	0.00	0.01
	9.25	1.21
	12.40	3.51
	13.38	7.60
	14.03	12.42

Frame 10' 3"		
X	Y	Z
3124.20	0.00	0.25
	7.54	1.73
	10.17	4.21
	11.13	8.12
	11.52	12.66

Frame 12' 3"		
X	Y	Z
3733.80	0.00	0.93
	4.55	2.98
	6.31	5.66
	6.79	9.25
	6.81	13.32

STONEFLY OFFSETS

METRIC Dimensions are millimeters

BOW		STERN	
X	Y	X	Y
15.08	28.58	284.96	5.56
91.28	34.13	286.54	30.16
92.87	8.73	362.74	24.61
152.40	14.29	364.33	50.80
228.60	23.81	346.87	76.20
304.80	39.69	304.80	76.99
330.20	48.42	228.60	82.55
355.60	61.91	177.80	94.46
372.27	101.60	127.00	123.03
370.68	127.00	112.71	152.40
362.74	152.40	113.51	177.80
334.96	203.20	132.56	228.60
295.28	254.00	165.89	279.40
231.78	324.64	199.23	320.68
174.63	322.26	134.94	323.85
203.20	282.58	101.60	275.43
228.60	242.09	50.80	214.31
257.18	177.80	19.05	152.40
261.14	152.40	7.94	101.60
261.14	152.40	12.70	76.20
254.00	119.06	25.40	62.71
232.57	101.60	76.20	38.10
177.80	87.31	152.40	21.43
101.60	80.17	284.96	5.56
50.80	75.41		
25.40	71.44		
13.50	50.80		

STONEFLY BRACKETS

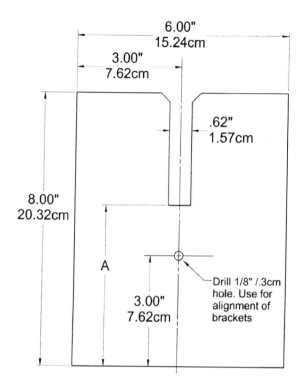

This shows the overall layout for each of the four brackets that attach to the strongback. The brackets locate the frames of the boat in the proper position. Once mounted to the strongback you attach the appropriate frame to the bracket.

The 5/8" wide slot needs to be just wide enough for the stringer to slide inside and not stick.

You may find that you need to trim the corners at the top to clear the stringers on the frame.

STONEFLY BRACKETS	
BRACKET LOCATION	**'A' Dimension**
FRAME 2' 0"	5 3/16"' (131.74 mm)
FRAME 5' 9"	4 1/16" (103.17 mm)
FRAME 8' 3"	4" (101.6 mm)
FRAME 12' 3"	4 15/16" (125.41 mm)

CHAPTER SIX

PREPARING FOR THE BUILD

TOOLS NEEDED

- 3' level
- Drill and bits (1/8", 3/32" diameter) for pilot holes
- Screw driver(s) or drill with screwdriver bit
- Wood mallet or a lightweight hammer
- #8 x 1 1/2" screws with washers

At this point you should have your strongback built and set up. Your stringers should be complete, frames cut and ready to install. If so, you're ready to start assembling the frame.

Before you start to install the frames, if you have not already done this, you need to sand them and check for any flaws. If you do find any holes, fill them with 5-minute epoxy. Once the epoxy is dry, sand the frames smooth, especially the inside edge where the lashing will wrap around the frame. An 80 or 120 grit foam sanding block is perfect for this.

ASSEMBLING THE FRAME

Start by installing the keel stringer in the slots in the brackets you previously mounted on the strongback. The keel should sit on the bottom of the bracket of the two on the ends. It probably will not touch the bottom of any brackets in the middle. That is not a problem; you will pull them down in place once you start installing the frames.

Locate the two end frames, place them over the keel and temporarily clamp them to the brackets.

Frame temporarily clamped to the bracket

MOUNTING FRAMES TO THE STRONGBACK

Find the two gunwale stringers, put them in the frames, and use your bungee cord to hold them in place. Don't worry about getting them real tight at this point. You just need to keep them from falling off.

On StoneFly I leave the gunwale strip off and install the stringer directly below the gunwale instead. The gunwales are installed last on StoneFly.

Bungees holding stringers in place

With the stringers held in place, lay a level across the top of the gunwales. Adjust the frame till the gunwales are level. Then clamp the frame to the brackets tightly. You will want a clamp on each side and you're going to need something that can apply enough force to keep it from moving. Spring clamps are not suitable for this. You will need something like a C or F clamp that you can tighten.

Once you have both frames leveled and clamped in place, it's time to drill a couple of pilot holes through the frames and into the brackets. The location is not critical; just center it in the frame and bracket behind it. Don't get too close to the edge of either one or it could break. Make sure the keel is all the way down and that the frame is properly seated on the keel strip before you drill.

Leveling the frame

I use an old Stanley 'egg beater' drill I keep set up for drilling pilot holes. Once they are drilled I drive in (2) #8 x 1 1/2" sheet metal screws with washers under the head to firmly clamp the frame to the bracket. If you prefer you can hold the frames in place with clamps instead of screws but they must be tight enough not to let the frame slip while working on them.

Drilling pilot holes

If you don't have the frame clamped tight to the frame brackets when you drive the screw in, it can push the frame away from the bracket. Make sure the frame is pulled tight against the brackets to avoid this problem.

Double check to make sure the frame is still level and still resting on the bottom of the bracket. Drill a pilot hole on the other side, insert the screw and washer and you're done.

Driving screws through the frame

Do the same thing to all the other frames that are to be mounted. Once they are in place, double check everything and make sure you have no problems.

Make sure the gunwales are level.

Check to make sure the frames are secure and tight against the bracket.

Confirm the brackets are secure to the strongback. You do not want any movement in the frame. If something is loose and moves, now is the time to fix it.

Check the distance between frames and that you put the frames on the correct side of the brackets. This is an easy mistake to make.

Lastly, tighten the bungee cords very tight! If you don't, in the next step you will end up with a pile of lumber on the floor. (You probably will anyway but this lessens the chances!)

ADDING ADDITIONAL FRAMES
(See next section for canoes)

You are now ready to install the rest of the frames. You should have your stringers held in place with bungees. Keep some extra bungees and clamps handy. It is likely you will want them in the next steps.

I like to start at the ends of the gunwales (bow and stern) and place a clamp on the stringers. This imparts a bow in the stringers and makes the assembly process a bit easier when you start to insert your frames.

A word of caution, **use common sense!** Don't clamp these too tight or you could break something. If you're not sure go slow. This applies to all of the construction. Wood will take a lot of stress but it will break if you overdo it.

Once the stringers are spread you can start inserting the frames in place. At this point I will typically measure and mark the rough location of the remaining frames. I don't worry about getting them in the exact position at this time. My goal is to get them wedged between the stringers, roughly located, wrapping extra bungee cords around the frame as needed.

Gunwale ends clamped

Fuselage Frame Kayaks

CANOE FRAMES

Installing the canoe frames is the same as installing kayak frames except for the gunwales. You should install the frames and then the stringers up to the gunwales. Leave the gunwales off for now, they will be installed later. Chapter Seven covers details on building the gunwales.

Since there is no deck tying the frames together, the frames can flex and if stressed enough they could break. To prevent this, I clamp a piece of scrap as a temporary thwart across a few of the frames near the top. A spring clamp is not strong enough so use a C-clamp or an F-clamp to hold the strip to the frame. I strongly suggest putting these on at least the centermost frames and the two frames closest to the ends.

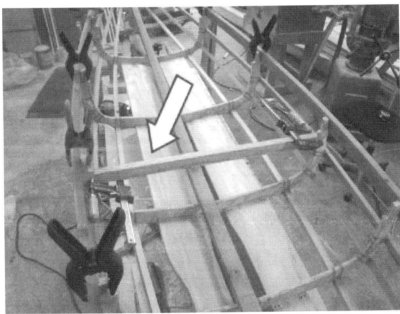

Temporary thwarts or bracing

As you're building the canoe if you notice a frame flexing you may want to add an additional brace. Pay close attention when installing the gunwales. There is a lot of force being applied to the frames as you build the gunwales.

ADD THE BOW ASSEMBLY

Once you have the frames installed insert the bow assembly in place and you can check the fit.

The stringer ends will look something like this where they meet the bow stem. On these I had a scarf cut on the end of the stringer but they need some trimming to fit properly. DO NOT just try to pull them in place with some clamps and skip trimming them.

TRIMMING THE STRINGERS

What you want to do is make a cut so that the stringer is parallel to the bow stem. In the photo the line is your cut line. You want to remove all the material to the right of the line, this applies to all the stringers.

The cut line

This will take some time and a good fit is very important. This is what yours should look like when you're finished. They don't have to be a perfect match but you do need a good fit.

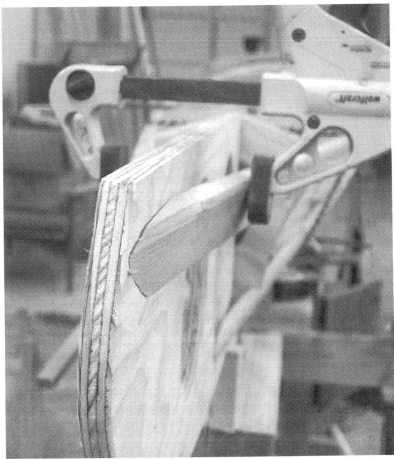

Trimmed stringer

There are a lot of ways to trim these. If you're good with a hand saw the quickest way is to clamp these in place, mark the cut and saw it. Clean it up with a rasp.

After trimming you may not have a good fit. I trim mine with a rasp or hand plane till they fit like I want. I started on these with a big rasp described in the tool section. I am pretty sure this is a farrier's rasp for shoeing horses. I love the large size.

Be sure to just file on the high spots, not the whole face. Remember you are trying to reshape the face so it fits flush with the bow.

Because the rasp leaves such a rough edge I like to take the block plane and clean up the faces. You can do this with the smooth side of the rasp and get it smooth enough. I use a lot of hand planes so this is more in my comfort zone. Just do whatever works for you.

Rasping the stringer ends

Using a block place to clean up the stringers

CHECKING YOUR WORK

Because the skin fits tight against the frame any flaws in the frame will show. If you have a stringer that doesn't fit correctly it is going to show and be very obvious! It's hard to see these looking at a naked frame so I take a piece of stretchy fabric such as old T-shirt and pull it over the frame to simulate the skin. This will give a very good idea of how it will look once it is finished.

Checking for flaws

Now is an excellent time to check your work and look for flaws. The bow is a location to check carefully as well as where all the stringers cross the frames. Stoop down and look down the gunwales and stringers from both the front and back and make the sure they bend in a smooth arc. If the curve is irregular find what is causing it. It could be that a frame is too far back or forward. You may have cut one of the frames incorrectly. If the problem is on one side only that is good indication of an error in the frame. Once or twice I have had a stringer that just didn't bend smoothly and I had to replace it. I used them on the deck or cut it for use as a seat stringer or deck beam.

STERN STRINGERS

On my boats with the Fantail Stern the stringers do not have to be trimmed to fit as they do at the bow. The stringers are trimmed a little long, so they extend past the frame.

I stretch the fabric over the stern and then decide what I want to do. Depending on the boat I may use an X lashing and trim the stringer flush with the frame. On some boats I can leave the stringer a little past the frame and lash it in the normal way. If the skin pulls tight against the end of the stringer, you may need to taper the end and/or round the end of the stringers so that you have a nice, smooth transition.

Just take your time and make it look good. It is a highly visible part of your boat and because of its unique shape it will attract a lot of attention.

Stern assembly

COAMING SUPPORTS

It's possible you will find that your coaming flexes too much when you're getting in your boat. If so, you can add a couple of brackets to support the coaming. They are epoxied to the frame and have to be cut to fit the boat. There should be a gap between the coaming and bracket and it should not touch the skin either.

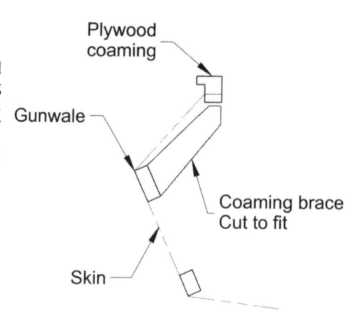

Fuselage Frame Kayaks

CHAPTER SEVEN

BUILDING THE FRAME

BUILDING THE FRAME

Finally you're to the point of tying all the frames together. There are two methods that you can use: lashing or "screw and glue". I advocate lashing but you have the option of screwing and gluing the joints together.

SCREW AND GLUE METHOD

I built one kayak using this method and while it worked I vowed to find a better way. (That is when I tried lashing and became a believer.)

While gluing the frame together worked, I really hated the experience for several reasons - the expense of the epoxy, the mess of working with it and the need to work quickly before the epoxy started to set up. Plus when I drove the screws into the plywood frame sometimes they split the plywood. After all that, you still have to clean up the epoxy runs and drips from the frame. As you can tell, I am not a fan of this method.

I know some people will not trying lashing regardless what I say so I will briefly go over this method.

To keep the plywood from splitting you need to drill a pilot hole through the stringer into the center of the plywood frame. It is very important to drill the hole in the center of the plywood. The size of the hole will depend on the size screw you use. I would suggest nothing larger than a #10 screw and I would probably use a #8 screw.

With the stringers clamped in place drill a pilot hole and then drive the screw in the plywood. There is very real possibility that the plywood will split when you do this so to prevent that you will need to clamp a block of wood on each side of the plywood while you drive the screw.

Go all the way around the frame, drilling pilot holes and driving the screws in. Once this is done you need to remove the screws and clamp stringers in place as you remove the screws.

For glue you will need to use thickened epoxy because of the gaps between the frame and stringers. Wood glues such as Titebond III need surfaces that mate together well and the stringers and frames do not have a good mating surface. Start on one end and pull the stringer from the frame and coat the mating surfaces on the frame with the epoxy. Drive the screws back in and be careful not to over tighten them. Keep in mind that the plywood can still split at this point. Make sure the screw heads are below the surface of the stringer. If they are not they could damage the skin.

I have never tried it but I have read that some builders will skip the screws and hold the joints together with nylon pull ties. If you can pull the joints tight enough I think this would be a big advantage over screws and much quicker.

LASHING

As George Dyson said *"The puzzle is not why did human beings start lashing things together, but why did they stop?"*

Lashing has a lot of advantages and so far I have not found any drawbacks. Lashing a joint is simple, if you can tie a knot and pull a string tight, you can lash a boat together.

If you lash a joint and then look at it and think, *"I could have done better"* or *"I made a mistake"* you simply remove the lashing and do it again.

There is no rush to finish before glue sets. No wasted pots of epoxy. No need to clamp each joint and no clean up. It's also great for people with limited time because you can quit at any time and pick up where you left off.

What about strength you ask? If you are using sinew with 70 lb breaking strength then 8 turns around the joint should take 8 x 2 x 70 lbs or 1,120 lbs of force to break the lashing. Plus the joint is not rigid so there is some elasticity that will allow it to flex, absorbing some of the energy. It is like a shock absorber built into every joint. I have built many boats this way and never had a joint fail.

LASHING STEP BY STEP

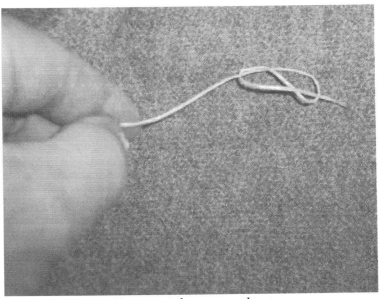

Figure eight stopper knot

First step with all lashings is to tie a stopper knot. Experience has shown me that the figure eight knot shown in the photo is preferable to an overhand or—as some call it—a granny knot. Waxed sinew is slippery and when pulled tight the overhand knot will slide apart. The figure eight knot has enough friction to stay tied. So always use it as your stopper knot.

Eskimo knot

All lashings will start with what Christopher Cunningham refers to as an Eskimo knot. It starts with the figure eight stopper knot and an overhand knot as shown. Pull the knot tight and slide it into place. You will want the knot on the inside of the frame so that it doesn't show under the skin.

Lashing the frame

Wrap the sinew around the frame a couple of times as shown and pull tight. If you are not straining, you're not pulling tight! You should pull the stringer

　Fuselage Frame Kayaks

into place against the frame.

Because the sinew can cut into your hand I use a piece of dowel a few inches long and wrap the loose end around it 3 or 4 times and pull on the dowel. As well as being easier on your hand it also gives you more leverage to pull the sinew tight.

Wrap it around the frame a couple more times and pull tight again. Sometimes you can see it 'bite' into the wood.

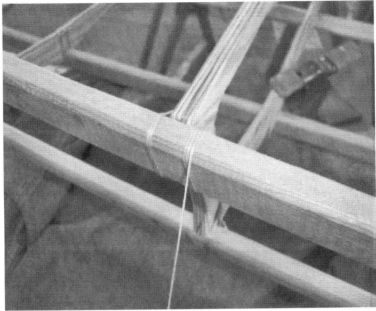

Another view of the lashing

To make your boat look more professional, when you start your lashings always start the lashing on the same side and tie them off on the same side. It doesn't matter which way you face them, just be consistent. It's a little detail but it's the little details that make an outstanding boat.

I wrap the sinew around the frame about 8 times. Then I take a small flat bladed screwdriver and CAREFULLY slide it under the sinew to lift it up enough to slide the sinew under itself. If you prefer, you can use a needle to feed the sinew through.

Create a loop as shown. Feed the loose end through the loop and pull tight and repeat.

Tightening the lashings

When you pull it tight you should pull the lashings together as shown in the photo pulling the lashings even tighter.

Don't be alarmed if it loosens up at first. Just keep tying these and pulling them tight by wrapping the loose end around your stick and pull tight. After 3 or 4 times it will stay tight.

Almost finished

After several repetitions of the previous step, this is what you should have. Now you need to tie this off so it will not come loose.

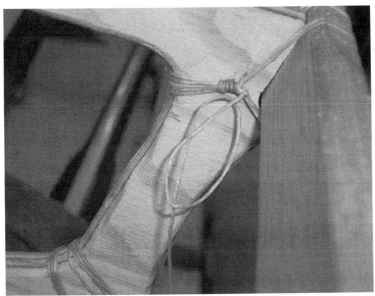

Stopper knot

To finish off the lashing you need to put in a stopper knot to keep it from untying itself. A simple overhand knot works here since there is no strain on the lashing. Just try to pull the knot down as low as possible to make it look neater.

LASHING THE KEEL

Lashing the keel is the same as the frames except for one small difference. If you just wrapped the sinew around the keel the lashing would leave a series of small bumps in the skin, which would always rub eventually wearing a hole in the skin.

To prevent this I file two small grooves in the keel for the lashings using a round rasp. The sinew will lie in the slots keeping them from being the low point on the boat.

Slots in the keel

Finished lashing

You lash the frame in place just like you do all the others. Here is how the finished lashing should look once it is tied off and trimmed.

THE Y LASHING

To lash a stringer to a bow (or stern) requires something a little different. It is called a 'Y" lashing because of its shape.

The Y lashing

On the bottom, you start by filing grooves under the keel strip for the lashing like you did for the frame to keel lashings. Then drill a hole in the plywood and lash though the hole and around the keel several times. Finish it just like you did the stringers; make several hitches, pulling the lashings together and forming the Y shape.

At the top you will drill holes through both gunwales or stringers depending on the boat. I clamp them in place till I have the lashing finished to keep them from moving and getting out of alignment.

THE X LASHING

In tight spots like a narrow bow or stern where there is limited space I will sometimes use what I call an X lashing.

X lashings

Wrap the sinew around two opposing stringers and pull the stringers tight against the frame. In the center of the lashing tie a series of hitches just as you did on the other lashings, pulling it tight forming the X shape. Your lashing should not look like an X till you tie it off in the center.

ADJUSTING FRAME POSITIONS

I start lashing at one end of the boat at a frame that is mounted to the strongback. I adjust it to make sure it is square with the keel and vertical with the strongback. To do this you will need to move the frames around to get them in the proper place.

I have found the easiest way to make a small adjustment is using a wooden mallet. You tap, not hammer, on the frame and that will usually move the frame a small amount.

Adjusting frames

If you find your frame is way out of position you may need to loosen the bungee cords to move the frame close to its correct position before you use the mallet.

Measuring frame positions

To check if the frame is square with the keel you need to measure from a point on the centerline of the boat. I place a pushpin or a small nail in center of the keel and hook the tape measure end over that. I measure to where the frame and gunwale meet. Both measurements should be the same. If the measurements are not the same then your frame is not square and you will need to adjust it some more.

As you're doing this keep using the framing square to check to see if it is in line vertically. Don't be surprised if you have go through this several times to get it right. It can be a slow process so take your time.

Once I get a frame located I lash it in place. Sometimes you cannot lash the keel because the frame is mounted to the strongback and the bracket. I lash all the other joints and once I remove the frame from the strongback, I go back and lash the joints I couldn't get to.

Once you have the first frame lashed in place, move on to the next frame. What I prefer to do is to lash the frame to the keel making sure it is in the right location, and I don't worry about it being square at this time. By lashing the keel, I have locked the frame in place. I move on to the next frame and do the same thing till I have all the frames lashed at the keel, except of course the mounted frames.

With that done, I will go back and start squaring the frames and lashing the rest of the joints.

Something to keep in mind is DO NOT measure from frame to frame to frame. Always measure the distances between frames from a common point. Typically I use one of the mounted frames. The reason is that if you make a mistake and have a frame in the wrong place, then measure from that frame to another one it is going to be in the wrong place and every frame after that will be wrong too. That is why I always measure from the same point. By measuring from the same place if I make a mistake I will only have one frame to move, not several.

CANOE TERMINOLOGY

Canoe terminology is a little different than kayaks so I need to explain a couple of terms. The gunwales of Stonefly are made of two strips of wood. The outer strip is called the outwale and would be outside the boat on a traditional style. The inwale is the inner strip, which would have been on the inside of the canoe. With fuselage frame construction they are both on the inside of the boat.

Another term you need to know is breasthook. This is a piece of wood that is fitted between the inwales. It adds strength to the ends of the boat as well as giving a more finished look.

CANOE GUNWALES

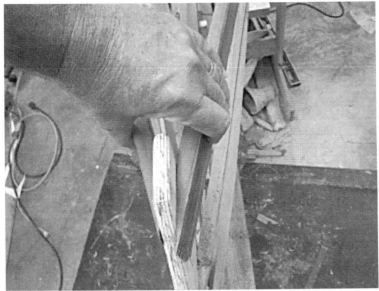

Trimmed outwale

Now that you have the frame lashed together it is time to build the gunwales. If you have not installed the temporary thwarts that I mentioned on page 79 do it now!

First step is to trim the outwale to fit the boat. You will need to clamp it to the frames while you fit it to the bow and stern plate.

Once I get that done I like to reshape the tops of the frames where the outwale touches the frame. These are cut square but the inwales are at an angle. So take a rasp and file the frame down to get a good flush fit since these will have to be glued instead of lashed.

INWALES

Inwales are next but they require that you know what you want in the way of breasthooks. I just attach mine on top of the gunwale because that is the easiest way. If you're a good woodworker you may want to fit yours between the inwales but this takes a level of skill most people do not have.

I suggest going ahead and roughing out the two breasthooks now. Then when you cut your inwales just make sure that they will end up under the breasthooks as shown.

Breasthook roughed out

The length of the breasthook can vary. Since this one was built for fishing I wanted the bow long so my fishing rod tips would be beneath it and lessen the likelihood of a limb grabbing one and pulling it out of the boat. This breasthook is around 20" and comes just past the frame. On the rear I used a much shorter one, but again, this can vary.

Once you have settled on the length of your breasthooks you can trim the inwales to length. It will not hurt anything if they are longer, just don't cut them too short!

You will need to shape the inside of the frames to mate up with the inwale just as you did the outwale.

Once I get the inwales cut to length, I clamp them in place and decide on what size I want the spacer blocks to be. Like the breasthook, the sizes are up to you. I like the look of a spacer block around 2 1/2" to 3" with 6 to 6 1/2" space between them. I try to space the frames in 3" increments to make the spacing easier for myself. If you add the spacer block length and the length of the space together and it is a multiple of 3 (i.e., 6", 9" ...) you should be able to use that without a frame ending up in the middle of a spacer block. For example you could use a 2 1/2" block with a 6 1/2" space between them. Then I take the time to dry fit them in place to make sure that it looks like I want and will fit properly.

Once you're satisfied, I suggest marking their location and then gluing the blocks and the outwale in place without the inwale. It is much easier that way.

Gluing spacer blocks in place

It will take a lot of clamps to glue these up so make sure you have enough before you start.

Once this dries I glue the inwale in place.

With the gunwales built you will need to flatten the top edge. The simplest way to do this is with a hand plane. Just keep working from end to end till you have the gunwale surface flat. Round over the inside edge and sand them smooth.

Be sure to allow for attaching breasthooks on the ends.

THWARTS

You will need to install at least one thwart in the boat. I went with two in my boat just to ensure there were no problems. It makes the boat frame very rigid. When you make your thwart don't just install a straight piece of wood, take the time to shape it a little. It will make the boat look much better.

Thwart

I located one thwart behind the seat where I could tie a cooler or tackle box to the thwart. It could be placed close enough to put a backrest against it. I placed a second one far enough in front that I could rest my rod on it but yet still slide it easily underneath the thwart.

Once you decide on the location, flip the frame over to install the thwart. I glue the thwart to the inwale and I also drive a couple screws in on each side (on the underside). Thwarts take a lot of abuse so you want it to be well anchored.

INSTALLING BREASTHOOKS

Breasthooks are highly visible and one of the first things people will see when they look at your boat. So you want to pick a nice looking piece of wood for this. It can be a solid piece or it could be several pieces laminated together. Just use your imagination here.

Breasthook clamped in place

In the gunwale section earlier in this book, I show an easy method for installing the breasthooks by just gluing them on top of the gunwales. These are structurally sound but they do not look as good as breasthooks that are fitted in place (if you have the skills to do that).

With the breasthooks built and roughed to size I start to fit them to the boat. Make sure that there is good contact with the gunwales so that you can get a good glue joint. At this point it is a good idea to go ahead and finish the back edge since it would be a little hard to do on the boat. I just put a simple cut out and round over the edge before installing. Be sure and clamp it well so that you have a good glue joint.

Trimmed to the gunwales

Once this has dried you will need to trim the breasthook. I go straight to my block plane and start working the edges down to the gunwale and bow stem. Round over the edges and make everything look nice and smooth, then sand it. I like to finish mine before I put the skin on since there is less chance of dripping something on the fabric.

I decided to just go with an oil finish on this one instead of varnish. It will probably take more upkeep but I should never have to strip it down to bare wood to refinish it either.

Finished breasthook

DECK BEAMS

Before you trim the deck beams to length you need to place the coaming on the boat and check the fit. Different boats have different methods of construction at the front of the coaming. Each boat is little different, but they all need to have coaming in place before you make the final cuts.

Single deck beam

Poco Barta and Curlew have a single deck beam. It is just a matter of leaving it long enough to be able to lash it to the frame and making sure the coaming can rest on it.

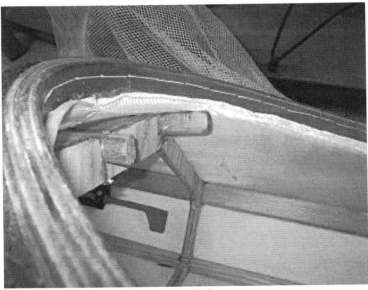

VARDO

VARDO, one of my other designs, has 3 deck beams that end at the cockpit. The center needs to be long enough to be able to lash it in place. The cockpit actually rests on the other two beams and they need to be longer. If you cut them short, the coaming will rest on the top of the frame or the center beam but the two deck beams will make ugly humps in front of the coaming. So always put the coaming in place before you trim the ends off the deck beam.

FLOORBOARDS

I started out gluing the floorboards in place with epoxy and I had one fail while sitting in it on the floor testing footrest positions. After watching the way

they bend with my weight on them I have once again decided lashing is the way to go. If an epoxied joint were to fail after the boat is together it would be really hard to repair. If a lashing failed you could relash it using a curved needle to feed the sinew.

Start by drilling a set of holes near the end similar to what is shown here. I

Lashed floors

suggest when you drill the holes you clamp a scrap piece of wood on the back side and drill into it. It will keep the plywood from splintering when the drill bit goes through. You will want to sand and remove any rough edges around the drilled holes.

Your lashing will basically be a straddle lashing similar to what you did when you lashed the keel to the frames and stringers to the ribs.

Tie off the lashings the same way as the keel. Try to do better than I did in this photo and tie everything off on the same side. It makes the boat look more professional when everything is consistent.

With some of the new

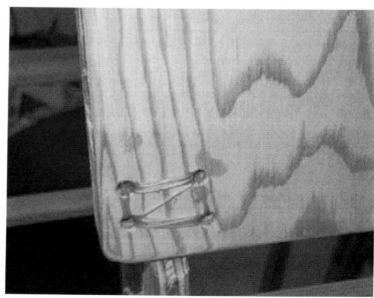

Bottom of the seat

designs I have started using strips instead of plywood for the floorboards. These are lashed in place just like the stringers are lashed to the frame.

CANOE floors are installed the same way. They are just longer and there are more holes and lashings.

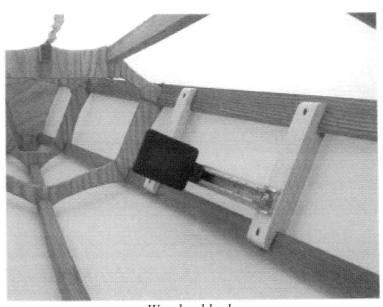
Wooden blocks

INSTALLING FOOTRESTS

Since Curlew is narrow at the feet I also found myself wishing I could move the footrests further outwards to gain a little more wiggle room.

After a lot of head scratching I came up with some aluminum brackets that accomplish both goals. They bring the footrests further to the outside and raise them up higher.

Regardless if you decided to make your own or if you buy the brackets, I suggest you clamp the footrests in place and see where you want them. Also if possible, measure an existing boat. I would suggest measuring from the back band (or back rest) to the footrests.

Since your boat is designed for the backrest to be 4" forward of the frame, add 4" to your backrest to footrest measurement, then measure that distance from the frame at the back of the cockpit to the foot pegs. Position

Frame is upside down in this photo

the footrests along the track so you have adjustment both forward and backward.

I am about 5' 8" and have average leg length and I locate the footrests centered on the track 49" from the back frame or 45" from the backrest.

Assemble one of the brackets to the footrest and position it on the stringer.

Checking for clearance from the skin

Lay a straight edge against both stringers and make sure that the screw head is not out past the stringers! If the screw head is past the stringer it will hit the skin of the boat. You can see in this photo I used a scrap of wood and laid it on the stringers.

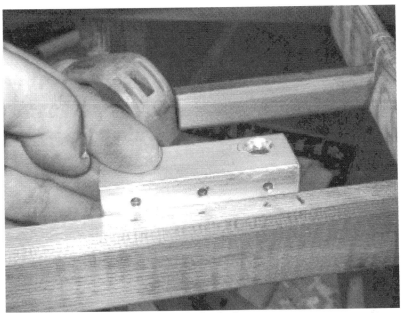

Mark the holes

Mark its position and then using the bracket as a guide, drill pilot holes for the screws. This is not easy because the lower stringer is in the way. Since you're coming in at an angle, don't drill these very deep. Just drill deep enough to get the screw started.

Once the first bracket is in place, I attach the footrest to the bracket. Put the screw in but don't tighten it fully. Put the second bracket in place with the screw and mark its location. Make sure the screw head is not out past the skin here too.

Then you can remove the screw and the footrest will just pivot upwards out of the way on the back screw you put in. Drill your holes, install the screws and bolt the footrests in place.

Now is the time to check the footrests and make sure they work properly and that they are in the right place! Once you put the skin on it's going to be very hard to change.

I put the frame on the floor with a blanket or a couple of rubber mats under it and sit in it. I adjust the footrests and make sure they work properly and that I can adjust everything easily.

PAINTERS

Rope painter

Next step is to drill holes for the painters. Painters are the loops of rope at the bow and stern of the boat. They serve as handles, a place to store one end of the paddle on deck, a tie off point on your car and more. What you do is personal preference since there are many ways you can make them. If you haul your boat on top of a vehicle painters are an excellent point to secure a bow line to the car.

At this point I drill the holes in the frame. Even if you decide you don't want painters, I would suggest going ahead and drilling the holes for them. If you change your mind you can open the hole in the skin and feed the rope through for the painters.

OILING THE FRAME

The last step before starting to skin the boat is to oil the frame to protect it. Most people recommend using pure tung oil on the frame. Some say that boiled linseed oil is food for mildew but that is what I have used and, so far, no problem. If you can find tung oil that is what I would suggest using.

Oiling tools

My method is to use a small disposable brush and just brush the oil on the frame liberally. I start coating the frame brushing everything I can see. Then I flip it over and get all the areas I couldn't see or have missed.

The oiled frame

As you can see, the oil changes the color of the wood and you can tell easily where you have oiled and not.

Fuselage Frame Kayaks

CHAPTER EIGHT

SKINNING THE FRAME

SKINNING YOUR BOAT

You're finally to the scariest part of the process - sewing the skin. For some reason the thought of sewing seems to terrify a lot of men yet sewing is actually a very straightforward process. But before you start sewing you need to decide on which fabric you want to use.

The method you use to sew on the skin depends on which fabric you choose. If you're using the polyester fabric with a loose weave I have produced a 3-part video on sewing this fabric. You can view it at kudzucraft.com, if you have a smart phone you can scan the QR code.

CHOOSING THE MATERIAL

Most people have a lot of anxiety about choosing which fabric to skin their boat with. There are basically three choices, only two of which I use.

I prefer to use either a nylon or polyester fabric. There are good and bad points to both fabrics but either one is a good choice and will make a good skin.

Many people cover their boats with a reinforced vinyl or PVC material. Most of these are reinforced with a cloth backing and are often a material intended for truck tarps. I think this appeals to people that are afraid of sewing because the fabric is glued together and the fact that there are some bright colors available. Many boats have been built using it and while no doubt it works, it never appealed to me so I have never used it. Most of the boats I have seen ended up with a lot of wrinkles in them. I don't think this material will stand up to abrasion very well and that is something most kayaks see a lot of.

Some have even skinned their boats with the clear unreinforced vinyl. This makes an unbelievably cool looking boat! It's great for showing off your wood work but it is not a practical choice. With no reinforcement you have to be very careful with it. A stick that would bounce off any other skin would puncture the clear vinyl. Plus it is like sitting in a greenhouse; it traps the sun's heat and is very hot inside!

NYLON

Nylon is the most commonly used fabric and it is probably the toughest. It is the one I choose if I am skinning a boat that will see a lot of abuse. Nylon's biggest advantage is that it stretches a lot. I have read that nylon will stretch 300% before it finally breaks. The ability to stretch is what makes it very puncture resistant.

Of course nylon is not perfect and has some drawbacks too. There isn't much that will stick to nylon, so your choices for waterproofing are very limited. If you want your boat a color other than white you have to dye the skin using an acid (vinegar) dye.

Nylon has one draw back that I really dislike; it is hygroscopic, meaning it absorbs water. When it does, it relaxes and will become loose on your boat. As a builder I don't want to sell a boat that I have to explain to the owner to expect the skin to go limp when it gets wet. No, it doesn't matter what you coat it with. It will happen regardless. From my experience, the heavier weight fabric like the 12 oz. material seems to loosen less than the lighter weight fabric, but they all loosen to some degree.

Some people wet the skin and keep it wet while they sew it. That way it is in the relaxed state when you put it on. I tried it once but it didn't make much difference for me, it still went limp once out on the water. Yet, I had a client that tried this and when the skin dried it shrank so much it broke a stringer on the boat.

Even with the drawbacks I use nylon on boats that may see some rough use because of its puncture resistance.

POLYESTER

For most of my boats I use a polyester fabric. I like it because it is stable and does not loosen when wet. The other thing I like is you can use most any oil based or water based finishes: paint, varnish, polyurethane, etc. Most polyester will heat shrink too and that is a big advantage.

Polyester is not as tough as nylon; it doesn't stretch nearly as much before the threads start to break and therefore it is not as puncture resistant. From what I have read polyester stands up to abrasion better than nylon. I think a typical kayak is more at risk from damage by abrasion from sliding over things than something hitting it and puncturing the skin. So even though it is not as tough as nylon, it doesn't mean it is not tough enough.

NEEDLES

I use two different needles. I use a straight needle for most of the stitching and I use a curved needle on the deck when sewing the whip stitch. You should be able to find upholstery needles at a fabric supply store.

THREAD

There are several options when it comes to the thread you use. I have read of people using dental floss, braided fishing line, braided Dacron, sinew and more. I have used the waxed sinew on several boats with no issue. I actually like the way it sews but not the way it looks.

I have started using a braided polyester twine that I like even better. It is supposed to have a 60 lb breaking strength and it is not waxed. I don't know what it was used for originally but it is similar to the braided fishing lines.

When it comes to thread use a synthetic so it doesn't rot and use something that will accept whichever finish you are going to apply to your boat.

STITCHES

There are two basic stitches you will use on your boat. The one you will use the most is the running stitch. The other stitch is the back stitch. The illustrations should explain well enough how to do both of these.

Running stitch

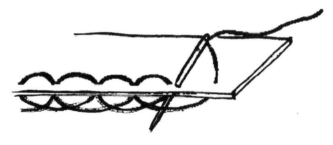

Back stitch

TRIMMING THE FABRIC

The best way to trim the fabric is to melt it with a hot knife. This leaves you with a good edge that doesn't unravel as you work with it. The only downside to a hot knife is that the good ones tend to be very expensive. Most people make do with a cheaper option. While it is very slow you can take a pencil style soldering iron and flatten the tip to trim the fabric. The higher the wattage of the iron the better it will work.

Pocket sewn on bow

Some of the larger soldering guns such as the Weller soldering gun have an optional cutting tip. I have used one of these for a long time and it's faster than the pencil style soldering irons but much slower than a real hot knife.

DRAPING THE SKIN

Start with the boat frame upside down on your work stands and roll the fabric over the boat leaving an even amount of material past both the bow and stern.

Starting on one end of the boat I find the center of the fabric by holding the two corners of the fabric together and pulling the fabric tight. This will give me its approximate center. I line it up with the keel of the boat and put a spring clamp on to hold it in place. Move to the other end of the boat and do the same thing.

From this point what you do next depends on which fabric you are using.

SEWING TIGHT WEAVE FABRICS

With the skin in place you will be sewing a 'pocket' over one end of the boat. You can start on the bow or the stern. In these photos I am skinning my Curlew design and I decided to start at the bow. Using a back stitch I sew around the bow forming the pocket. I prefer the back stitch at the bow and stern because these areas will have a lot of tension on them and the back stitch is a stronger stitch than the running stitch.

Start at the bottom of the boat and sew upwards toward the deck. Keep in mind the boat is upside down while you're doing this. Where to start sewing is just a matter of judgment based on the fabric you're using. Pull the fabric snug and around the bow. Keep in mind the higher up the bow you start the more fabric you will have to stretch out to avoid a wrinkle in the skin.

I prefer to have the seam start as high as practical so I can add a wooden rub strip on the bow. Also, every time I beach the boat I don't want my seam to be hitting the bank. Unfortunately I can't tell you where yours will start; it is just one of those things that you have to work out on the boat.

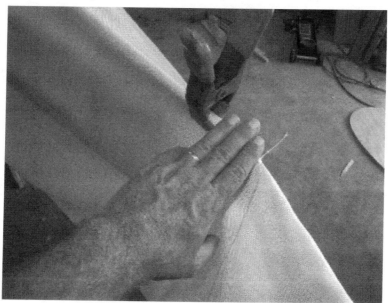

Measuring 3 fingers width back

Once the pocket is sewn on the bow move to the stern of the boat. You want to pull the fabric snug down the center of the boat keeping it centered. I use a spring clamp to hold it in place. Determine where you need to start sewing just like you did at the bow.

On Curlew I find that the seam on the stern has to start very close to the bottom to prevent wrinkles forming further up. Once I determine where I need to start stitching I insert my needle to mark the point. <u>Remember where this point is on the frame</u> since you are going to move the skin and will need to slide it back.

I measure from the start point I just marked toward the bow 3 fingers width (that is approximately 2¼" - 2½"). I move my needle to mark this new spot. This is where you will start sewing the second pocket on the boat.

Go to the bow of the boat where you have previously sewn the pocket and slide the pocket off the boat. Slide the skin back so that the new position of the needle is lined up at the starting point on the frame, then clamp the skin in place so it doesn't move.

Sew around the stern just as you did on the bow, except you do not want to go all the way around at this point. You just want to go to the point that the frame starts to curve backwards, just far enough so when you stretch the skin

Fuselage Frame Kayaks

over it doesn't slide off. The further you sew the harder you are going to have to stretch the skin and it is hard enough to stretch as it is.

On a Fantail stern this is just a short way up the stern as shown. You can see where it starts to curve back. On a Greenland style boat with a long overhanging bow you would have to go all the way to the deck.

Once you have the stern pocket sewn, slide it off and put the bow pocket back in place.

Next, you are going to stretch the skin and slide it over the stern locking it in place. I will warn you this is not an easy step! It may take two people and it will test how well you lashed the frames. You did pull those lashings tight, didn't you?

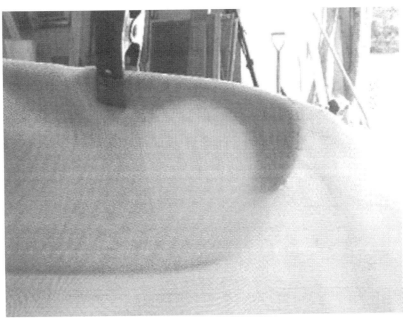

Stern of a Curlew

I find it easier to put the frame in the floor and slide my feet under the boat, bracing them against one of the frames, then pull the skin tight and slide the pocket in place over the stern.

When you brace your feet against the frame make sure you put your feet near the gunwales and not in the center of the frame! If you don't you could break a frame.

This is a good time to have a second person to help pull because as I said it can take a lot of effort to make the fabric stretch far enough to get it back on the boat. There will be a lot of tension on the skin and if it slides on easy you didn't do it right.

Once you have the skin in place, it is a good time to take a break. I like to pull the skin down over the middle of the frame and double check to make sure that I didn't miss anything. Make sure that the skin lies flat and there are not any bumps or other problems. If you missed something you really want to catch it now since this is your last chance to correct any flaws.

If everything looks good I start inserting pushpins (thumbtacks) down the keel to hold the fabric in place while I sew it on. I place them approximately every two feet. This is very important. Do not skip this step!

SEWING THE SKIN

Push pins in the keel

If you are working on a boat with my Fantail stern it can be a bit tricky, and assuming this is your first boat it's better to start at the bow and get some experience sewing. Otherwise it doesn't matter, but you may want to start at the stern. I think most people look closer at the bow of a boat than at the stern.

Since you are using a tightly woven skin you have to pull the skin tight on the boat with the stitches. This requires stitching a large gap and then using the mechanical advantage of the thread(s) and pulling the fabric together down the middle.

Batten clamped in place

I slide a thin 3/4" wood batten down the center of the boat and use it as a guide to place my stitches in the fabric. I pull the fabric tight over the batten and insert my needle along the edge of the batten.

Then I switch to the other side, pull the fabric tight and using the batten as my gauge put in another stitch along the opposite side of the batten. Every few stitches I pull the thread tight. This should pull the fabric together and tight around the boat. I find that it is easier on the hands to wrap the thread around a dowel or scrap of wood and pull on that.

Every few inches you need to stop and check your work and make sure your seam is sewn tight. Take both sides of the fabric where you're stitching it together and pull them apart and look at your seam between the two pieces of fabric. You should see the fabric pulled tightly together. If you see a gap between the fabric, you're sewing is too loose. If you haven't gone too far you can usually pull hard on the thread and close it up. If it doesn't pull together you will probably have to remove a few stitches, pulling it tight.

Figure eight knot on painters

As you're sewing the skin don't forget to install your painters. Once you get the skin on tight and past the holes you drilled it is a good time to do this. While you can do them later it is much simpler to put them in now as you go along. Once the skin is tight you can heat up a nail or something similar and make the hole in the skin where you drilled the hole in the frame.

If you have not drilled your holes for the painters do it now!

If you decide you don't want painters the holes will not hurt anything and it is much harder to drill the holes with the skin on.

Fuselage Frame Kayaks

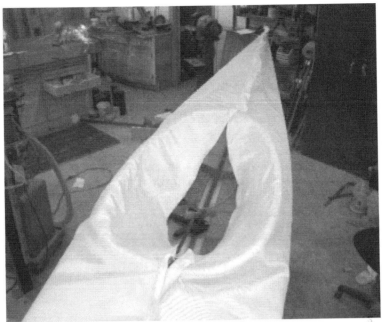

Coaming ring in place

If you are using the stacked plywood coaming you want to put in the lower coaming ring before you sew all the way to the cockpit. I suggest temporarily lashing it in place. Or you can clamp it but I find the clamps tend to get in the way.

Make sure you put the ring in right side up! Double check the fit with the coaming and mark it before installing it. Otherwise they are not going to line up properly with the top half. (We'll get back to the coaming shortly.)

Sewing a Loose Woven Fabric

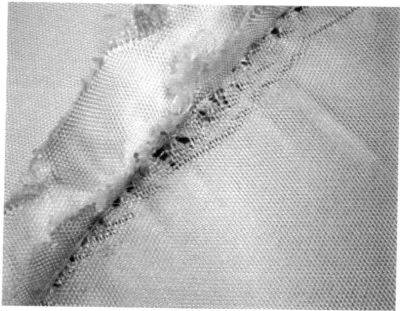

Pull holes

If you're sewing on a loose woven fabric like the polyester you'll have to use a different technique than with a tightly woven fabric. You cannot pull it tight with the stitches or you end up with lots of holes in the fabric as shown in the photo. You must sew the skin on rather loose and then shrink the fabric tight.

Start with your frame upside down on the stands. Roll the fabric on the boat and center it so you have about as much fabric hanging off the front as the back of the boat. Standing at one end of the boat, find the center of the fabric and clamp it to the boat. Move to the other end, find the center, pull it snug and clamp that end.

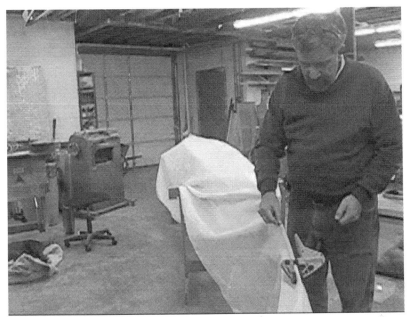
One end clamped

Next, insert a row of pushpins along the keel spacing them approximately 1½' to 2' apart. Make sure the fabric is centered over the keel and not twisted.

Roll the boat over. If you are using the plywood coaming you need to put the bottom ring in place now. Make sure it is centered and I suggest you temporarily lash it in place so it doesn't move. You will cut the lashing later.

Start in the center and gently pull the fabric snug around the center of the boat and clamp the skin in place working toward the ends. The idea is to pull the wrinkles out and help prevent the skin from twisting on the frame.

If you are using a laminated coaming place it on the boat to determine where it will rest on the frame. I start sewing the skin at a point that will be just inside the cockpit.

Clamping the fabric

SEWING TIPS

There are a couple of tricks to sewing the skin on. I use the center deck beam as a guide, sewing down the center to keep my stitching straight. If the boat doesn't have a center beam then slip a thin wood strip in and use it as a guide, removing it once you are finished sewing.

When you're sewing the fabric you want to keep the fabric clamped to the gunwales, this helps to keep the skin from sliding on the boat. You will need to move the clamps around as you sew.

When sewing, pinch the fabric together so that both pieces are touching where you run your stitch. You do not want to tug the fabric toward the bow or stern of the boat at first, just towards the center.

You will want to lift the fabric upward off the deck beam. I have found that I get my best results by just pulling the fabric between my fingers on top of the deck beam and making my stitches almost flush with the beam. Make sure both sides of the fabric are touching or you will end up pulling the fabric together and creating pull holes.

Regularly pull the loose ends of the fabric apart and look at your stitching. It should be tight with no gaps. On the outsides there should be no big pull holes. Small ones are normal but try to keep these to a minimum. If you are getting a lot of larger holes that means you are pulling the fabric together instead of it being together when you sewed your seam. Never be afraid to take out your stitching and start over. I have been doing this a while and sometimes when I check I have to remove some of my sewing and do it over.

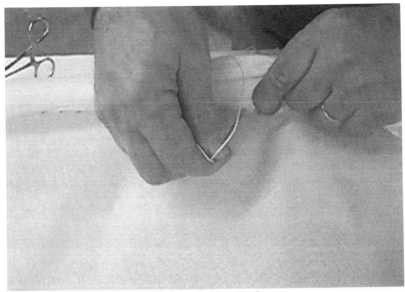

Stitching the deck

From the cockpit I will sew about 6" and then I will put a spring clamp on near where I started sewing and clamp the fabric to the frame. This will keep you from pulling the fabric forward as you sew the rest of the seam.

About now I will trim off some of the excess fabric. I leave a good bit more than I need at this point. I just want to shorten it up so I don't have so much fabric to deal with while I am sewing. I trim the fabric leaving at least 4" past the deck beam. When you start to cut one side be sure the other side is not under your hot knife.

Now that the skin is clamped to the frame, when I pinch the fabric together I can pull it forward too. This sounds trivial but it is important in keeping the fabric even on the boat.

Watch for anything more than a small wrinkle forming as you sew and periodically stop and check to see if you are twisting the fabric on the boat or pulling one side further forward than the other. The skin should be a little loose on the frame but it shouldn't be baggy, either.

When you reach the bow, continue the stitching around the end at least a little way to form a pocket for strength. Depending on the bow shape you may have to go well around the bow to finish off the sewing.

Right before I make the turn at the bow I switch to the back stitch since it is stronger. Once you shrink the fabric there can be a lot of tension at the bow and stern.

INSTALLING THE PLYWOOD COAMING

With the skin sewn in place it's time to install the coaming. You should have the bottom coaming ring under the skin. Make sure it is in the correct position and centered from side to side. If you lashed it to the frame leave the lashings in for now.

Coaming clamped in place

You may want to trim some of the excess fabric from the inside of the coaming ring about now. Then fit the upper coaming ring on the lower, pull the fabric snug and clamp the two together.

Before inserting the screws, you need to create a hole in the fabric for them. Otherwise the screw can grab the fabric and pull a run in it. You can take a small Phillips screwdriver and insert it in the holes. This should create a small hole in the fabric for the screw.

If you have a safe way to do it you could melt a small hole in the fabric but there is always the risk of a fire or damaging the skin. I have heated a nail, held it with pliers and slipped it in screw holes.

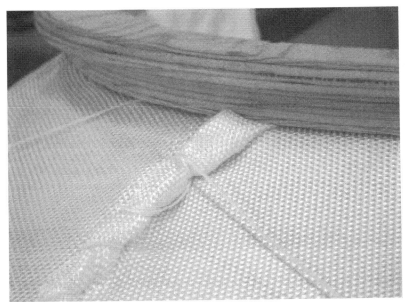

Deck seam at coaming

Once you have your hole in the skin drive in a screw. Alternate from side to side pulling the fabric snug and being careful to work out any big wrinkles. As you tighten the coaming pieces together you should be clamping the skin tightly between the coaming pieces locking it in place.

The seam down the deck creates a bit of a problem. What I do is trim most of the fabric off as close to the edge of the coaming as I can. I will leave approximately ½" of fabric past my stitching under the coaming. I will apply some caulking around this area before clamping it together. That will seal any holes that might be left around the fabric.

Last step is to trim the fabric flush with the inside of the coaming.

INSTALLING THE SEWN-IN COAMING

Your coaming should be finished before you start to install it. Start by placing the coaming on the boat then use a tie down strap wrapped under the boat and over the coaming. I tighten the strap a little to hold the coaming in place while I locate where it should rest.

Clamping the coaming

Once the coaming is in place I pull the strap tight, then I pull it even tighter. The idea is to actually deform the coaming so that it is under tension with the strap holding it in place. You sew the coaming to the skin and when you release the strap the coaming tries to snap back into its original shape, tensioning the fabric

Once you have the coaming in place make sure it is centered on the boat. Next I trim the fabric so I can start stitching. I pull the fabric against the inside edge of the coaming and trim it flush with the top edge of the coaming. This leaves the right amount of fabric to fold over but not be left hanging out from under the coaming.

Finished coaming

Fold the fabric over with the cut edge on the inside, against the coaming so that it is hidden. Pull the fabric snug and start stitching. Watch for wrinkles as you sew.

Sometimes I will take small nails and push them through the fabric to temporarily hold it in place. I will go all the way around the cockpit putting a nail in every 2nd or 3rd hole. As I sew I will remove them.

You will sew around the coaming twice. If you have an odd number of holes in the coaming you will make two passes around the coaming and it will bring you back to where you started. If you have an even number of holes drilled in the coaming you end up right where you started. So you will have to stitch backwards one hole so you can fill in all the gaps with the thread.

Once you have the coaming sewn in place you can release the clamp.

SEWING A CANOE

Sewing the skin on a canoe starts out just like sewing the skin on a kayak. You sew the pockets on the ends and stretch the fabric over the canoe. Follow the kayak instructions; just keep the following in mind:

- If using nylon you need to sew pockets like on the kayak. You may want to do this with the skin wet since nylon relaxes when wet.

- If you are using polyester sew it on dry.

- I drape the skin on the boat and clamp it in place along the gunwales like in the photo.

- Be sure and insert the push pins (thumbtacks) down the keel line. The pushpins are very important!

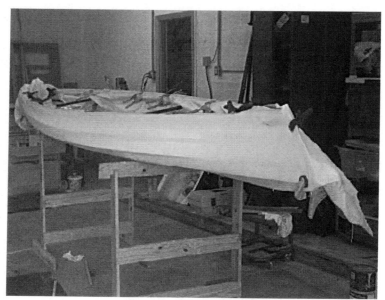

Skin clamped in place

STAPLE THE CANOE SKIN

Once the ends are sewn you need to attach the skin to the gunwales. I staple mine in place with stainless steel or Monel staples. You can install these with a regular staple gun or an air powered model if you have an air compressor. I have been using a SureBonder 9600 stapler. The price is very reasonable and it gets very good reviews. So far I am impressed with it.

You need to have decided what you want for a rubrail at this point. (More about rubrails in the next section.) I cut the rubrails and then take a small piece of the rubrail to use as a gauge.

Before I start stapling the skin onto the boat I have pulled the skin in place and clamped it to the gunwales as shown in the previous photo. I start in the center of the boat, drive a few staples and go to the other side and do the same thing. If you're working with nylon, pull the skin as tight as you can and keep it wet. I keep working towards the ends of the canoe. I use the piece of rubrail to check and make sure that my staples are going to be covered when it is installed.

Next step is to finish the ends with a whip stitch and trim the skin. I end my whip stitch by just making several stitches similar to a lashing as close to the breasthook as I can. Then I use the hot knife to cut and seal the end.

I strongly suggest you apply your finish before installing the rubrails.

CANOE RUBRAILS

Rubrails serve two purposes, trim to hide the staples and to prevent damage to the skin. How and where you plan on using your boat should help you determine what to make them of. The more abuse they may see the more important a tough hardwood will be. Since I am pretty easy on mine I decided to use cedar.

You can make your rubrails any size you like but I think narrower rub rails look better than big bulky ones. I like something around 5/8" to 3/4" wide. Drill screw holes to attach the rubrails approximately every 6". You want to countersink the heads of the screws so when you hit something it hits the rubrail and not the screw head. Otherwise it could pull out the screw and damage the boat.

When you drill the countersinks I suggest using a depth stop of some type so your holes are consistent and when you drive in the screws they will all look the same.

When you install the gunwales apply caulking between the rubrail and the boat. This will keep water from entering behind the rubrail and allowing the rubrail to rot. Plus the caulk will keep water from entering the gunwale through the screw holes.

FINISHING THE SEAM

There are a couple of ways to finish the seams on the boat. I like the whipstitch. The whipstitch is pretty simple and quick to sew. Plus I like the look of the finished stitch; I think it helps to hide crooked seams.

Step one is trimming the fabric to length. I like to trim the two edges 1 ½" long. I will cut a piece of wood to the right width and use it as a guide so that I cut the fabric the right height.

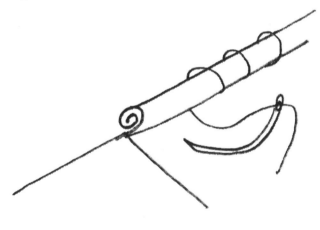

Whipstitch

Take the excess material and roll the fabric down and run a stitch under the rolled fabric, and then over. I like to make my stitches about 1" long. When you pull the stitch tight you should end up with a pattern that looks like a twisted rope.

Finished whipstitch

I work from the ends of the boat toward the coaming. To end the stitch I trim my fabric as close to the coaming as I can and I make several stitches right together and then tie it off.

SHRINKING A POLYESTER SKIN

The safest and recommended way to shrink the skin is using a clothes iron. I strongly suggest you test it on a piece of scrap fabric before you apply it to your boat. I believe polyesters have a lower melting temperature than nylons. So always test the iron on a scrap piece of fabric to make sure it's not going to melt the material and it is hot enough that the fabric actually shrinks. Leave the iron in place for a minute or so just to make sure it's not going to damage the skin. It's much better to find out on the scrap piece.

Once you have the temperature set it is a simple matter of applying the iron to the skin and slowly working it around the boat. I start on the top and then flip the boat and work on the bottom. You can do it either way, as it really doesn't matter.

You can also shrink the skin with a heat gun but be warned; **YOU CAN MELT THE SKIN!** Heat guns get very hot and I have tried it and literally melted the fabric. Sometimes I use one but have to be really careful and NEVER let the gun stay in one spot. You must keep it moving constantly. Even doing that you can overheat the fabric. I only mention this because I know someone will get impatient and grab the heat gun. *If you ruin your skin you have been forewarned!*

CHAPTER NINE

FINISHING THE SKIN

WATERPROOFING THE SKIN

Now that your boat is skinned you have to waterproof it. If you use the nylon or polyester skin it is not waterproof so you have to coat it with something. Which fabric you choose will determine which waterproofing you can use.

Many finishes will not stick to nylon. Polyester fabrics will take most anything. But just because it will stick does not mean it is a good finish. You need a coating that is as flexible as the skin or it will eventually crack. There are several options for coatings and no one perfect coating.

White skin with ZAR

NYLON FABRIC

For nylon, ZAR <u>oil based</u> Exterior Polyurethane is an old standby that has been proven over many years and many boats. I have been surprised at how well it has held up to abrasion. I have run my boat across rocks, lots of submerged trees and limbs. So far I haven't had to touch up the coating. It just has a few marks on it. After about 4 years of hard use I am just starting to see a couple of areas on the bow where it bumps onto stuff that it may need some touch up pretty soon. The rest of the boat looks really good.

The one thing I don't like about Zar is it will change your white skin to an amber looking color. If you want color, ZAR can be tinted with pigments used for oil based paint. I have my local hardware store tint it for me. Once tinted it's still translucent instead of a solid like paint. Also, it is hard to get a dark color with just ZAR because of this. Reds can end up looking pink, so be careful if you go this route.

Another good finish for nylon is Dura-Tuff polyurethane. It is hard to find and it is a rather nasty smelling product but it creates a very tough glossy finish. It is water clear and if you want a white boat this is a good choice. It can be used over dyes too. I think it would make a good choice for a white polyester boat skin too.

If you want a solid color you can dye the skin using an acid dye such as Jacquard acid dyes and color the skin before you coat it.

There are several other finishes that I have not tried that I have heard good things about. Epifanes Spar varnish is one of them. It has a great reputation in wooden boat circles for bright work.

Skin Boat Schools/SpiritLine's 'Goop' is a popular coating. It is a two part urethane that has been modified chemically for use on kayaks. It is supposed to adhere to nylon very well and makes a tough yet flexible coating.

Being a two part coating it is critical to get the mix right. It is not brushed on but poured on the boat and then spread with a squeegee. You apply three coats, one after another while it is still wet. You must watch it close so you can touch up any runs or drips. If you apply it too thick, I am told it will foam. Everything I read implies it is not an easy coating to use your first time.

Coelan Marine coating is supposed to be one of the best coatings for fabric due to its extreme flexibility and great durability. I have heard it was rather expensive but I haven't seen reliable information on the prices. It sounds like it has the potential of being an exceptionally good coating and should work well on polyester too.

POLYESTER FINISHES

One of polyester's advantages is that most anything will adhere to it. This opens up a lot of different finish options.

Rustoleum oil based paint has been one of my favorites for polyester. I have used it on several boats and I am well pleased with the results. It will take 3 coats of paint to seal the skin. I have tried to do it in 2 coats but I always find 'pin holes' in the fabric when I shine a bright light through from the opposite side.

The one downside to Rustoleum is the lack of color choices and the glossy finish. The gloss shows all the flaws and if you apply paint a little thick in a small area it really shows. This means you need to pay attention to the details when you're applying the paint.

I have recently started going to a paint store and having my colors mixed. I just ask for their best exterior oil based enamel paint. If you want to have some fun tell them what you are painting.

If you are going to use paint I suggest a semi-gloss or even a flat finish. It looks better over the fabric than a glossy coat over the textured fabric.

I tried water based (latex) paint after reading the experimental aircraft web sites. Many of these guys are advocates of water based paint so I decided to try it myself. It worked and it is a viable option but honestly I was not impressed. I found it harder to apply because it didn't flow on evenly like oil based paint. Plus is took more coats of paint to seal the skin. Water based takes a long time to dry, I have read it takes up to 4 weeks to fully harden. Some articles have said even longer than that.

After several months of drying it is still nowhere near as tough as oil based enamel and scratches fairly easily. It's easy to touch up however.

Even though I don't like it much it does have some good points. I love the water clean up! There are no harmful fumes so you can paint indoors and water based paints are not flammable. So don't dismiss water based paint.

APPLYING THE COATING

Curlew being painted

Before you start coating the boat you need to make sure the boat is clean. If you were careful while skinning it may just need brushing. Sometimes there will be a mark on the skin that may need to be cleaned.

If you ended up with larger pull holes in the skin there is a way to deal with it. It's not my first choice but you can use Lexel caulk to seal up small holes. Lexel is a great product for this purpose. You can apply a small amount to holes and level it out. It's messy to work with so just use a very small amount.

Sometimes you will have a hole that you think the paint will fill and after the first coat you find it is still there. I will apply a small amount of Lexel and once it dries I apply another coat of finish to the boat. If you were careful and didn't over do it, no one will know.

Be warned a lot of builders frown on this with good reason. It's not a replacement for good craftsmanship. It is much better to do it right the first time and this is basically a patch.

Most coatings can just be brushed on using a paint brush. I have always preferred bristle brushes for painting. Recently I have been using 3" wide disposable foam brushes on my boats and I am starting to like them better.

I have also used the 3" or 4" wide paint rollers. Not the 1" diameter rollers, but the larger ones like a standard paint roller. I can apply paint quicker with these than a brush. I often follow behind with a foam disposable brush to even out the coat.

I am going to give you my best advice for painting with a brush; do not overload the brush! Most people get way too much paint on the brush. You want to dip the brush in the paint a little bit. You should not have to struggle to keep paint from dripping everywhere. Paint is meant to be applied in multiple thin coats. Thick coats only lead to runs.

Using oil based enamel paint over polyester I have found that 3 coats rolled on and then brushed will seal the hull. You can get away with 2 coats on the deck but it will probably allow water to seep in so I go ahead and do 3 coats.

If you have spray equipment you may want to spray the finish on the boat. This works especially well with ZAR.

I strongly suggest practicing on the scraps left over from skinning your boat. You may want to build a simple square frame and stretch and staple some scrap on it and experiment. I will stress the point once more, Don't Rush! The water will still be there tomorrow.

Here is a tip on testing your boat before you go in the water. Once you think you have enough finish on the boat, put it outside on some sawhorses and get it fairly level. Then dump a couple of gallons of water in it and see what happens. If you have done a good job, nothing. If not so good, you will see some water drops on the outside of the boat. Lift each end so that water fills the bow and then the stern and watch for leaks, especially at the seams. They are typically the hardest areas to seal.

Fuselage Frame Kayaks

CHAPTER TEN

THE FINAL DETAILS

RIGGING YOUR BOAT

By this point you're so close to taking your boat to the water it's probably killing you. I know when I get a new boat to this point I am ready to go to the water too.

Start with your deck rigging. What you do here is personal choice, so think about what you are going to do with this boat and that will help you decide what you need and how you want your boat to look. About the only thing I keep on the deck is my spare paddle. In the summer I may keep a bottle of water or my waterproof binoculars. In the winter, I may take off my gloves and stow them under a line. Since I don't carry much, I go with simple crossed deck lines.

Toggles

On a boat that is not that stable and might be a little hard to get in and out of I may install toggles. These work best if you use rope instead of bungee. You slide your paddle underneath with the toggles in the center. Then you spread the toggle out which pulls them tight onto the paddle holding it against the deck. That gives you sort of a kickstand to steady the boat. If you're using an unfeathered paddle the blade against the water will slow down the movement of the hull and makes getting in and out much easier. In shallow water you can even lean the boat over till the blade hits bottom. Attaching lines to the deck is simple. I like to use nylon webbing with a stainless steel screw and upholstery washer to make the anchors. A short strip of webbing is cut to length. You need to melt a small hole for the screw to pass through. I use a hot knife to melt the hole but you can hold the nail with pliers or drive it in a piece of wood and then heat it. Whatever you do, be careful! It will burn your skin as well as burn a hole in the skin of the boat!

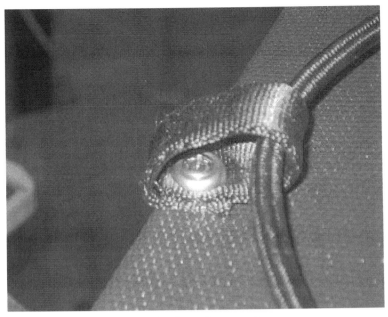

Finished tie down point

Put the screw through the holes as shown. This way the head of the screw is mostly hidden giving the deck a little cleaner look.

When installing these, I suggest you measure from a common point on the centerline of the boat, like the tip of the bow to the point you want to mount the anchor. If you measure from the same point for each one, they should line up evenly.

I make pencil marks and then I drill a small pilot hole in the skin where I want to drive the screw. Be sure that you are centered over solid wood! I do not recommend driving screws into the frames but rather the gunwale along the edge.

Then carefully drill a small pilot hole in the stringer. You may want to put a straight edge (ruler or scrap of wood) on the side of the stringer to make sure your drill goes in straight.

I apply a small amount of Lexel caulk around the screw on the nylon strap to keep any water from coming in and then tighten the screw. Repeat this process around the boat, tying off

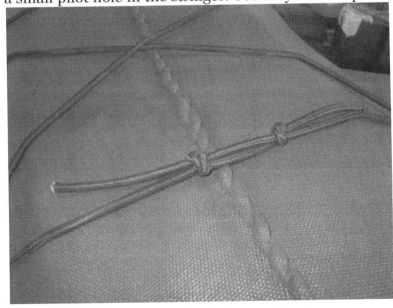

Deck lines with a fisherman's knot

the bungee.

This style of anchor can be used for lifelines as well. A lifeline is a line that runs around the perimeter of the boat that gives you a way to hold on to the boat should you capsize. Without it there is little you can grab onto.

When installing bungee cords I have found a couple of simple overhand knots work as well as anything. (This is also known as a fisherman's knot.) I tie off one on one side with the loose end pulled through. Then I pull the bungee tighter than I want and tie the second knot as shown in the photo. Then slide the two knots together, trim the ends and it is done. Check the tension before trimming off the end and make sure it is not too loose or too tight.

PAINTERS

Painters are the loops or handles on the ends of the boat. They are often used to tie the boat to the car with bow and/or stern lines. Therefore, it is important to install these right. I will assume that you have drilled your holes in the frame before getting to this point and that you have not installed them as you skinned the boat. If not, you're going to have a hard time drilling them and not damaging the skin

There are many options as to how to make painters and this is a good time to get creative. Here are a few ideas.

This painter was made from ¼" diameter rope which is too small and will cut into your hands. It was doubled up and a decorative series of square knots were tied making it more comfortable.

Braided painter

Another method would be to use a 3-braid line and splice the ends together by braiding them. Whatever you do make sure it is secure and will not slip if you are going to use it to tie to your car.

If you paddle where there are big waves, you shouldn't have a loop of rope but a toggle handle instead. If you have your hand in the loop and a wave rolls the boat, it could trap your hand in the loop. A toggle handle will just twist around and not trap you to the boat.

Simple loop painter

INSTALLING A BACK BAND

Installing a backband is quick and easy. Feed the bungee through the bottom loops on the backband first. Then feed them under the frame and back over the top of the frame.

Bring the ends of the bungee through the two top loops and tie it in the center using the same two overhand knots you used on the deck line.

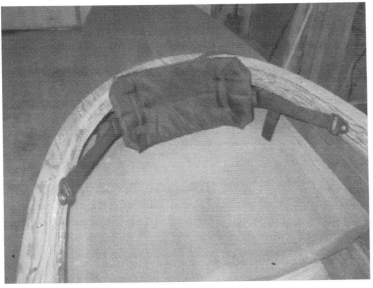

Installed backband

Next you need to decide where you want to mount the straps. You don't want to go too far forward or the straps will pinch around your waist. Mark where you want the screw holes and drill pilot holes in the coaming. Be careful not to drill all the way through! Then insert the screws (and washer if needed). Be sure and caulk around the screw to prevent water from entering and allowing rot to set up in the wood. Once the straps are installed you can adjust the bungee on the backband. All of our boats are designed for the backband to be 4" in front of the frame under the rear of the coaming.

The last step is to install a seat. There are a lot of options and seating is a personal choice. Without a comfortable seat, you're not going to use the boat for long. I have found the mini-cell 'tractor seats' to be the most comfortable. You can buy the foam and carve your own. I prefer to buy a preformed blank that I trim to fit my boat.

Your boat is ready to take to the water for its first paddle but there are still some things you need to do.

FLOAT BAGS

Most commercially produced boats have bulkheads and watertight compartments in the ends. Usually people assume they are just dry storage and flotation. However, they serve another purpose- they limit the amount of water that can get inside the boat if it capsizes.

Since skin boats do not have bulkheads they can hold somewhere around 3 times as much water. Being made largely of wood they typically will still float but emptying all that water, especially in deep water, is a major problem. Float bags help by providing flotation and greatly limiting the amount of water that can get

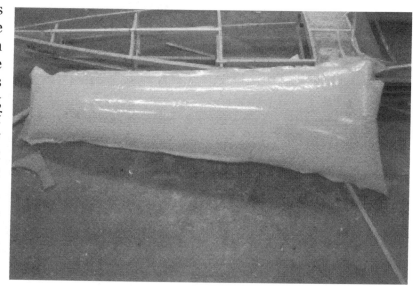

Float bag

in the boat. This is why I consider float bags essential items.

You can purchase commercial float bags or make your own. I have made them from heavy weight clear vinyl purchased at a fabric store. I glue the plastic with HH-66 glue. Glue in a length of vinyl tubing and use a valve on the end.

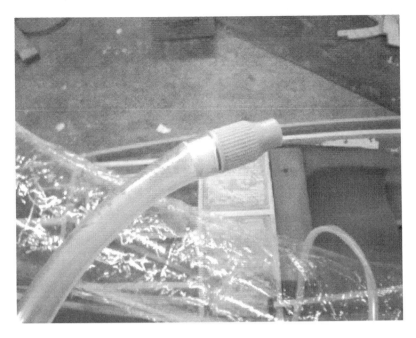

The drawback is the vinyl is not as durable as I would like but it is easy to patch using the HH-66 glue and a small piece of vinyl scrap.

Another option is using heat sealing nylon. You place the two coated faces together, run a hot clothes iron over it, bonding the two faces together forming an airtight seam. The nylon is more durable than the vinyl and more trouble free. However it is much more expensive than vinyl.

NRS valve glued on vinyl fill tube

WEAR STRIPS

The bow of the boat usually receives the most abuse and will start to show wear the quickest. Adding a wear strip to the bow is something I highly recommend.

I made wear strips from wood scrap in my shop for a long time. I cut small strips of whatever scrap hardwood I had in the shop. These worked well but after a while they started to look bad and eventually would need to be replaced. Recently I started using plastic for the wear strips because they last longer, although I admit they don't look as good.

I buy large plastic cutting boards used in the kitchen, cut it into strips, drill and countersink screw holes, apply caulking to the underside and attach it to the boat. This makes a very durable and cheap wear strip.

Plastic cutting boards can be cut with most any type of saw and you can use hand planes without damaging the blade and the best part is they are cheap. The only downside is since they are white they can really stand out on the boat. I find them rather ugly but I love the protection they provide and that is a good tradeoff.

The size of the wear strip is not critical. I like to keep mine on the small side and I usually round over the edges. This helps to keep the water from making a gurgling sound when paddling.

When you lay out the screw holes space them 2" or maybe 3" apart. Be consistent in the spacing, so if you need to make a replacement you don't have to drill new holes in the boat.

Be sure you drill the countersinks deep enough that the screw heads are below the wear strip. You want the wear strip to hit, not the screw head.

Wear strip

CARING FOR YOUR BOAT

With just a little upkeep you can greatly extend the life of your boat. The most important thing you can do is never store your boat wet. Always drain the water out and keep it dry while it is stored.

A tight fitting cockpit cover is a good idea, it can keep out bugs, spiders, and animals. Just make sure the boat is dry before installing the cover if it is to be stored for any length of time.

Next to water the worst enemy of your boat is the sun's UV rays. The finish on your boat will help to protect it but eventually the UV rays will break down the finish. If you store it in the sun you will have to redo the finish often to keep the boat in good shape and there is much greater risk of damage to the boat.

Dirt and sand will get in your boat and it is not always easy to get out. The best way I have found is to place the boat upside down on saw horses and use a garden hose inside the boat. Most of the dirt will wash out the cockpit opening. Sometimes I will put water in the boat, add some soap and let it soak for a while before rinsing.

If you paddle fresh water you will want to prevent any wood destroying fungus from setting up in the ends of the boat. I like to periodically rinse my boats with a gallon of water with a little bleach mixed in. I let it sit for a while in the ends of the boat since that is the most likely area to develop a problem.

Check the finish on the boat periodically to see if there is any damage that might need a little attention.

GREENLAND PADDLES

Every boat has to have a paddle and most people will just purchase one. However I think your boat deserves something better. My favorite is the Greenland style paddle, often referred to as a GP. Since you have built your own boat I suggest you do some research and consider building your own GP.

The Greenland style paddle design is believed to be thousands of years old. How this design came about is just speculation and we will never know for sure, but the one thing we do know is that the design works or it wouldn't have been used for so long.

The early Arctic paddlers were hunting for food on frigid waters, exposed to all kinds of weather and sea conditions. Their lives depended on their boats, paddles, and their skills with them.

The first thought most people have is "How do those skinny blades have any bite on the water?" Most assume that a GP will slow them down but that is not true.

The only time I have found I don't like a GP is in very shallow water. Because of the narrow blade it's hard to submerge enough of the blade to work well.

Greenland Paddles

ADDENDA

SUPPLIERS FOR PRODUCTS MENTIONED

The products, brands and companies recommended are not an attempt to promote that product. They are listed to assist the reader and any recommendations are our opinion. The author has no financial interest in any of the companies listed below.

- **ZAR oil based polyurethane**. This seems to be hard to find for many people. I have found it on the Do-It-Best-Hardware web site, www.doitbest.com. You can order on their web site and pick it up at your local Do-It-Best affiliated hardware store.

- **Colean** Their web site is www.coelan.com. Premapro, in Charlotte, North Carolina, www.premapro.com, is the only North American distributor for Colean. No experience with this product but it comes highly recommended from those that have used it. I understand it is very expensive.

- **Hot Knife** for cutting fabric. HSGM www.hsgmusa.com I use their HSG-0 Heat Cutter. It is a solid built tool that has served me well.

- **Valves for float bags.** The only place I know of that sells these is NRS. www.nrsweb.com

- **Heat seal nylon.** Rockywoods as well as Seattle Fabrics have a good selection of heat sealable fabrics. Rockywoods http://www.rockywoods.com
Seattle Fabrics www.seattlefabrics.com

 The author, Jeff Horton, is the owner of The Kudzu Patch Inc., which does business as Kudzu Craft Skin Boats. You can find Kudzu Craft online at www.kudzucraft.com. Scan the QR code with your smart phone to learn more about Kudzu Craft.

Kudzu Craft offers

- Full size plans for skin boats
- Supplies such as artificial sinew, fabric, footrests, backbands, etc.
- Precut kits and complete boats

We hope you have enjoyed this book and found it useful. In the process of writing this book I have discovered how hard writing a book is. It's nearly impossible to make it perfect. If we find any major errors, corrections will be posted at www.kudzucraft.com/books

These and other boats are available from Kudzu Craft

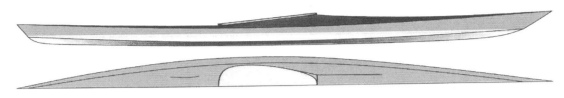

Ravenswood 15' long 24" wide

Ravenswood is based on the proven Curlew hull. I took what I learned with Curlew, tweaked the hull and improved it some. It has a little better performance in the 3-4.5 mph range than the Curlew. That makes it a good choice for most paddlers. The shorter length makes it easy to store and easy to handle. It should weigh in around 23-28 lbs with an 8 oz skin and western red cedar stringers. Scan the QR code with your smart phone to learn more.

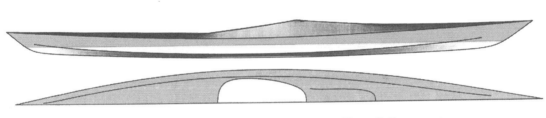

VARDO 17' long 24" wide

When I created my design goals for VARDO I made a list based on postings in several kayak forums. I kept seeing basically the same want list for a boat, around 17 feet long, stable and enough storage for some weekend camping.

VARDO is a medium volume boat that you can spend extended periods of time in comfortably. It's easy to move your legs into a new position so you don't cramp up. If you want to do some camping, add hatches and it would be a good touring boat. Its volume isn't so large that you're not going to be comfortable using it as a day boat either. I have used this boat for fishing. I loan it to new paddlers. I use it on the lake. It's just a good performing all around boat. Scan the QR code with your smart phone to learn more.

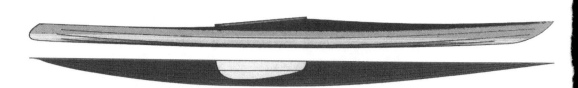

Short Shot 16.5' long 23" wide

Short Shot is the little brother of Long Shot. It is basically a scaled down version of the Long Shot hull. It has the multi- chined (round) hull shape instead of a single hard chine, which lowers the resistance and makes it faster and easier to paddle. The styling maintains our unique Fantail stern but has a pointed bow. Short Shot has a Stability Factor of 93. It should feel more stable than the number implies. If you have a smart phone you can scan the QR code to learn more.

FireFly 18' long 22" wide

I have always loved the looks of the Baidarkas. I had drawn a couple based on traditional designs and was just never happy with the results. They looked great but they were small and not very stable, not the kind of boat the modern day paddler would be happy with. FireFly is my version of a modern day Baidarka. It is not true to the 'traditional' Baidarka design but is very much inspired by them. From the bifurcated bow to the stern it is obvious where the inspiration of this boat comes from. FireFly is an easy paddling boat with good manners and good speed potential. If you have a smart phone you can scan the QR code to learn more.

INDEX

Fuselage Frame Kayaks

17422620R00083

Made in the USA
Charleston, SC
10 February 2013